ROTATION

Jones

1-10/14

Dorris

2/1/15

Happy
Camp

2/1/15

Yreka

10/1/15

Ft. Jones

/ /

EVERYTHING IS WONDERFUL

SIGRID
RAUSING

EVERYTHING IS WONDERFUL

*Memories of a Collective Farm
in Estonia*

Grove Press
New York

Maps copyright © 2014 by Martin Lubikowski

Published simultaneously in Canada
Printed in the United States of America

FIRST EDITION

ISBN: 978-0-8021-2217-9
eBook ISBN: 978-0-8021-9-2813

Grove Press
an imprint of Grove/Atlantic, Inc.
154 West 14th Street
New York, NY 10011

Distributed by Publishers Group West

www.groveatlantic.com

14 15 16 17   10 9 8 7 6 5 4 3 2 1

To Hans and Märit

Contents

Preface   1

One: The Collective Farm   7
Two: Former Owners   17
Three: The Russians   31
Four: The New Reality   40
Five: The Mercy of God   61
Six: History   71
Seven: Dear Comrades   96
Eight: Winter   122
Nine: Normal Life   140
Ten: Everything Is Wonderful   161
Eleven: Swirls of Dust   180
Twelve: Summer   197

Afterword   211
Timeline   217
Acknowledgments   221

North-Eastern Europe, 1989

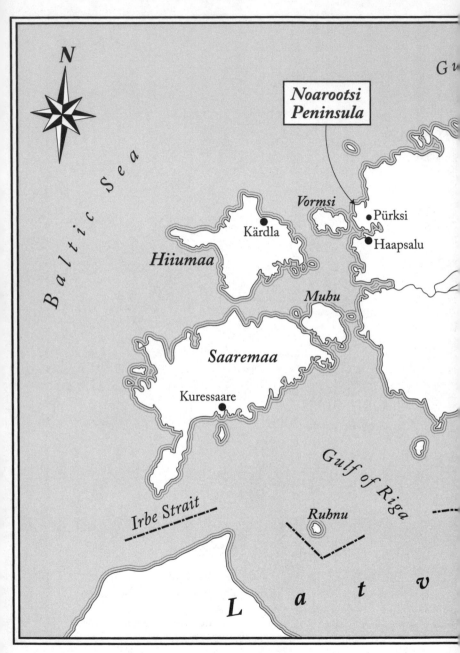

THE REPUBLIC OF ESTONIA

Finland

LINN

●Rakvere

Narva●

Russian Federation

●Paide

stonia

Lake Peipus

Tartu●

Võrtsjärv

●Võru

10   20   30   40   50 miles

EVERYTHING IS WONDERFUL

Preface

I have a photograph in front of me from the winter of 1993: a dilapidated barn stands on a snow-covered field, the blue and faint orange of the afternoon sky reflected in the snow. The field is in Estonia, on a former collective farm in a remote area on the west coast. The barn looks isolated and slightly melancholy on the vast field, having survived war, land reform, collectivisation, and, now, privatisation. The photograph is one of many. I also have a diary, and many letters and notebooks.

I lived on the collective farm for a year in 1993–94, gathering material for a PhD in social anthropology about history and memory. I was there to study the local perception and understanding of historical events in the context of the Soviet repression and censorship of history. I wanted to understand how the people on this peninsula understood their history, and how the war and occupations had affected them and their families. My PhD became an academic book, *History, Memory, and Identity in Post-Soviet Estonia: The End of a Collective Farm*, published by Oxford University Press in 2004. Parts of that book are replicated here. It was based on those same notes and the diary, though purged, of course, of anything personal. I make reference to Orwell in that book and in this, and the same characters appear through the pages. I hesitate to say that this book is more authentic—the real account of what actually happened—since scholarship was as much or more a part of my experience of being there as the daily life in this story. Much as my academic book excluded the personal, this book excludes the academic, but anyone who reads both will see that they overlap to some degree.

Estonia went through a war, and occupations—first by the Soviet Union and then by Nazi Germany—so devastating, and so violent, that nearly a quarter of the population had fled, disappeared, or been killed by the end of it. The population declined from 1,136,000 people to 854,000. Nor did the violence end with peace: the terror and repression continued in the second Soviet occupation. The mass deportation from the countryside in March 1949 was timed to weaken resistance to the planned forced collectivisation. My collective farm, encompassing some twenty villages and most of the land on the peninsula of Noarootsi, was formed shortly after the deportations. It was officially closed down in February 1993, following a vote by all the members in which just one person voted for its continued existence.

I had moved to England from Sweden in 1980. Part of my interest in this particular area was that before the war, some half of the people on the peninsula had been Swedish-speaking, belonging to the Swedish minority of Estonia. The Estonian Swedes lived on the west coast and on the islands they had lived there since the Middle Ages, fishing, trading, and farming. In 1944, in the dying days of the Nazi occupation of Estonia, the majority of the Swedes, some seven thousand people out of a total population of eight thousand, were evacuated by the Nazis. The Swedish government paid a fee per person to the Nazis, and saved the Swedes from the coming Soviet occupation, but the deal was, of course, tainting, and the refugees were encouraged not to talk about it, and to assimilate in Sweden as best they could.

In the early 1990s, on Noarootsi, you could still sense the effects of the evacuation, and the ravages of war and deportations. It was a bleak and depopulated area. Pürksi, where I lived, was the only village on the peninsula that had slightly increased its population since the census of 1934. All the other villages had declined dramatically, the largest shrinking from 480 people to 59, the smallest from 69 to 16. The total population was no more than a few hundred people.

The peninsula had been a Soviet military border protection zone, with limited public access. It had a permanent army base, and there was only one road out to the mainland, patrolled by soldiers on duty by a barrier. The barrier was still there when I arrived, but the soldiers were gone. Before independence, people crossing to the peninsula had to show their papers at the barrier, no matter how well known they were, or how often they crossed over. The coast was heavily guarded. At regular intervals along the whole coastline there were watchtowers with powerful searchlights. In some places people were not allowed access to the sea.

When I first visited Pürksi, in April 1993, there were some signs of progress. There was a new shop, and the church, the vicarage, and the manor house were being restored with funds from abroad. There were, also, many signs of post-Soviet decline. The communal dining room had been closed down, as had the crèche; the weekly cultural programme had been cancelled, the cold and dusty culture hall was empty, and there was little heating or hot water. The ruling Isamaa ("Fatherland") coalition was, people said, "building capitalism." People endured the sacrifices, with not much hope for the future, much as they had when the state was "building socialism." Poverty, and drinking, shortened lives, especially for men. Life expectancy in 1994 dipped to sixty years for men and just under seventy-three years for women. By 2012 it had increased to about sixty-eight and seventy-nine years, respectively.

The centre of Pürksi was a dusty square formed by the school, where I was to work as an English teacher, the culture hall, and the old workshops at the far end. At the back of the culture hall was Gorbyland, the basement bar named after Mikhail Gorbachev, whose attempts to curb the pervasive Soviet alcoholism were considered mildly amusing. There, also, was the rubbish dump; a pile of plastic bags torn apart by the village dogs, lit by a single bleak floodlight at night. There was a new little cooperative shop near the workshops. By the road coming into the village was the dairy, defunct since the 1970s, and the old Soviet shop, selling household stuff as well as some food, pots and pans, exercise books, shoes if they got a consignment, and ancient Russian jars of jams and pickles with rusty lids and falling-off labels. On the wide, low windowsill the alcoholics sat and drank in peaceful camaraderie. The atmosphere was quiet, almost somnolent.

The rest of the villages on the peninsula—bedraggled collections of grey wooden houses with thatched roofs, sometimes propped up by shoddy white brick—were like villages all over the Soviet Union at that particular time: forgotten places sinking into quiet poverty. There were dusty unpaved roads dotted with flaking milk stands, and many abandoned farmhouses slowly decaying in the forest. The poor and the old—people who may have been happy about independence, but for whom the winds of privatisation brought only loss—were bewildered. I can see them now, men and women with blank eyes and black teeth, old shoes stuffed with paper, shuffling slowly through the new supermarket in Haapsalu. The extreme sink or swim austerity of post-Soviet Estonia was ravaging at that time.

I stayed for a year. In the end, I was profoundly relieved to leave, and yet I also sometimes day-dreamed about staying on in that grey and tired modernity. It was so peaceful. People's idea of post-Soviet security was to lock their doors, leaving the key in the outside lock. There was no crime and, in fact, no reason for the *kolkhozniks*, the collective farm workers, to steal from one another, since no one had anything much to steal. I am not suggesting that it was idyllic—the poverty was harsh, particularly in the cold winter, and although independence (1991) was welcome, most people were impoverished by the changes. The Soviet welfare state, such as it was, had collapsed. Vaccinations and dental care were in disarray. Children's shoes were virtually unobtainable, and if you could find them they cost a month's salary or more. The Estonians had become free, but they were much poorer, and they couldn't then know how temporary that poverty was to be. They were suspicious and antagonistic towards the Russians, but some still talked wistfully of the old days, of hitchhiking across the Soviet Union, and of now-derelict summer camps and holiday resorts. By 1993 independence fervour had died down. The Singing Revolution, as the Estonian independence movement was called, was over. People hunkered down, drank, and endured.

My lasting impression of the collective farm now, so many years later, is of a deeply seasonal community. In the spring, there was an intoxicating sense of opening up, and the realisation that what had preceded it had been a state of near hibernation. The outside again became a public and noisy meeting place after the dark and snow-bound silence of winter. The summer was relentless in its own way; a long heatwave of glaring sun and dry wind day after day. There was a constant dust cloud on the square, and the men burnt to a dark reddish brown, delineated by their shirts. I sat on my shoddy little balcony in the heat, drinking salty Russian mineral water. It could have been some poor 1950s Italian suburb. The bar by the empty harbour had opened, and the season of white nights and drinking had begun.

When I finally left I took with me the glass bottle I had used for milk. For a year I had brought it to the shop, and had it filled it from the steel bucket of milk kept under the counter. I didn't think of it as a souvenir; I genuinely thought it would be useful, but of course I never used it again. I also never opened the cans of sprats I brought back, or drank the now long-lost parting gift of medical spirits. I finished my PhD whilst teaching undergraduates in the department of anthropology at University College London. I published my book based on the PhD, and many articles. I gave talks at conferences and seminars, until I married and had a baby, and drifted into another life.

Now, twenty years later, I am thinking about that strange year again. What was that, that long time of note-taking, of conversations, of writing and teaching in the school? I remember long and dreamy walks through that evocative and tragic landscape, those familiar northern forests. I thought often about Sweden, and about leaving the country where I grew up. There was a slightly punitive sense of doing time, of counting the weeks. But the intellectual stimulation of the discipline of doing fieldwork was intense. I wrote incessant notes, jotting down whole conversations verbatim. I thought, I read.

What was it? I don't know. I was doing fieldwork, but I was also just trying to get by. It was what it was. It was interesting.

ONE

The Collective Farm

In mid-August 1993 I was ready to start my year of fieldwork. I had bought an old Volvo in Sweden, ordinary and reliable, or at least I thought of it as ordinary. On the collective farm, of course, it looked like an ambassadorial limousine amongst the few rusty old Ladas. I had everything I thought I could possibly need, most importantly my new Mac laptop and a camera. I didn't bring a mobile phone, and, of course, there was no Internet on the collective farm, though I did have an early email account in England. I brought, instead, a little travel printer, and many rolls of printer paper. I had medical supplies, a down duvet, several pillows, books, clothes, pens, and notebooks.

I travelled across on the ferry to Tallinn, Estonia's capital, from Stockholm, as I had done many times before. I drove straight down to the collective farm. It was a sunny day, with a strange clarity of light. I drove west from Tallinn, past the small settlements of Keila, then Rummu, and a ruined monastery. I remember birds singing, and crossing a stream of brown water. The light shimmered strangely—there were mirages over the pockmarked tarmac. A rooster crowed in the silence between the few thundering lorries on the otherwise empty road. There was a hallucinatory quality to that drive. The loose flap of a lorry canvas in front of me seemed like an ominous message, the landscape drenched with meaning and expectation. I see now, so many years later, how alone I was, and how apprehensive.

The land on both sides of the narrow road into the peninsula was marshy. You could see that this had once been an island, or even several islands. I drove past some old grey houses with frayed thatched roofs and shoddy white brick additions, past the abandoned Soviet watchtower and barrier, now permanently propped open. I stopped at the church, built where the marsh ended. In the spring it had been locked up, in a state of disrepair. Now it was open, with newly painted grey benches, broad flagstones on the floor, spare and Lutheran. The guest book on the table by the door was almost full—there were sixty pages of names, most of them Swedish, the rest Finnish. The day before I arrived the Uppsala University theological faculty had visited. Next to the guest book was a pile of contemporary Swedish church tracts, perhaps left by the theological students. I looked at the titles: *Teach Us to Pray, Take Us into Your Joy* and, slightly glib in this harsh historical context, *You Will Not Abandon Me*.

Instead of driving towards Pürksi, the village where I was to live, I took another road, towards the sea, delaying the moment of arrival. It was a wide dirt road, and I drove on for miles. Outside each farm stood a wooden stand for the milk cans, though the dairy collections, I knew, had ceased for the time being, along with so much else. At the end of the road, by the sea, was a single abandoned white brick building, perhaps a family house, in that Soviet state of dilapidation that could signify incompletion or abandonment, or perhaps both. An open door was banging in the wind, and you could hear the waves. I wandered down to the beach. There were wheel tracks in the sand, but no one was there. Some round boulders in the grey sea were reminiscent of refugees, bedraggled families looking west across the water. I looked at them for a long time, only half aware of my reluctance to enter the village of my field site, meet my informants, and commit myself to my fieldwork, and to this year. Eventually I picked myself up and left, a subconscious mantra ringing in my ears: *Now is the time for all good men to come to the aid of the party*. Where did that come from? It was running endlessly on a loop through my mind. I didn't know then how safe I would soon feel—at that point I was anxious, not only about meeting people, but also about finding my way in the new field of post-Soviet anthropology.

Anthropological fieldwork is unlike any other occupation. You live and work alongside your informants in a process called "participant observation"—you participate, observe, record, compare, and analyse. As in psychoanalysis, research is often grounded in the seemingly inconsequential, in habitual references and jokes, revealing fragments of the worldview of the informants. It is generally assumed that the underlying worldview is a coherent imaginary universe, with its own internal logic, though "fieldwork at home" or "near at home," with people who largely share our cosmology, usually addresses more specific issues, in my case the questions of history and memory.

I am sorry to say that I didn't have much of an idea of what fieldwork was before I started it. My department at UCL was one of the best in the United Kingdom, and, probably, along with Chicago, in the world. We had had a great deal of theoretical training from famous experts in the field; we read, wrote, and discussed voraciously, but we had almost no actual training in field technique—the unstated thinking was, I suspect, that making it on your own enhanced the experience and the process of understanding and analysing the culture. I remember the traditional annual seminar for all the prospective PhD students in the presence of the whole department. We presented our fieldwork proposals, one by one. The Africanists were always particularly tough, and one student proposed to study diamond smuggling in Sierra Leone. This was before the term "blood diamonds" had been coined, but the extreme brutality associated with the diamond trade was well known. There was a thoughtful silence after he finished reading his lengthy and theoretically rich proposal, after which the chairman of the department asked, "And how do you propose to survive your fieldwork?" Everyone laughed. Now I think of that proposal, and that moment, as capturing the spirit of the department. We were on our own, deliberately so.

I was lucky, however, in my supervisor, Daniel Miller, an already eminent, now-famous anthropologist, and an energetic and encouraging correspondent. "You seek to comprehend both yourself, your own society, and the society you are studying in one movement," he wrote to me. "Doing fieldwork is also a process of gaining maturity and coming to a sort of bearable but rather stronger form of self-consciousness. At least that was my experience." And so it turned out for me. The process of cultural analysis was not dissimilar from the process of my psychoanalysis the years before my fieldwork, only more intense.

The road was much as it had been on my first visit in the spring. I passed the old shop on the right, and some white brick blocks of flats on the left, and arrived, finally, at the central square. "Square" is perhaps too urban a term for that dusty, long rectangle delineated by the school on the short side, the rusty workshops at the far end, the collective farm culture hall on the right, and the municipal offices on the left. I parked the car and cautiously stepped out. The square was empty. The glass in the door of the shoddy white brick culture hall was broken, and inside the bare concrete staircase was chipped and dusty. Behind were the collective farm apartment blocks, long two- and three-storey blocks housing some three hundred people. It was very quiet.

As instructed by letter, I went to report to the mayor, whom I knew by name as Ülo Kalm. He was seated at a modern desk opposite his assistant, tall and thin, dark and lively, and much younger than I had expected. They greeted me briefly, and immediately started looking in drawers for the key to the visitors' flat, the so-called hotel where I was to stay. The key was missing, so they started to call people to find out where it was. They each had a telephone, the mayor a Swedish modern one, his assistant an old Soviet one, and both phones were soon ringing incessantly with news of the key. The Estonian voices from the telephones were loud and clear, and the mayor and his assistant consulted each other constantly as they spoke, creating a strangely cinematic atmosphere. After a number of such telephone conversations, sadly still difficult for me to follow despite my lessons in Estonian, the mayor went off in person in search of the key. Silence descended; strangely even the telephone calls instantly ceased. I felt a little dazed. The assistant got me a cup of black coffee with eight chocolates lined up on the saucer. I sat in the peaceful silence, drinking the coffee, absent-mindedly eating the dry chocolates one by one. Ülo eventually came back without they key but with the information that the woman who had it would be back on the four o'clock bus from Haapsalu. He smiled encouragingly, and I left, saying I would come back later.

Diagonally opposite the culture house stood the dilapidated wooden manor house of Birkas, which had been in Swedish owner-ship before the First World War. There was no relationship between the Swedish-speaking peasants on the peninsula and the aristocratic owners of the manor house and estate. A few of the landowners in Estonia were Swedish, but most of them were Baltic German. Not many Estonians, many of them former serfs, or Estonian Swedes, owned land before independence. The baronial estates were first attacked in the 1905 revolution. In the post-independence land reform of 1920 they were broken up, and the land was parcelled out to returning soldiers.

That same year, the manor house of Birkas was turned into a boarding school for Estonian Swedish young people, to teach them new farming methods, to help them become "capable, moral, and forward-looking individuals," and to preserve the Swedish culture and language. Teachers and villagers restored the house themselves, with the help of the students. In the first year, the school took in thirteen boys and twenty-six girls. All in all, nearly six hundred students were educated at Birkas, more than half of them girls. What previously had been islands of Swedishness—small, isolated rural communities—became a self-conscious minority. The students were taught what was known as "Sweden Swedish," but were also encouraged to appreciate the "cultural value" of their own dialects. Soon a steady stream of Swedish visitors, journalists, filmmakers, and representatives of charitable societies visited the Swedish communities in Estonia: a Swedish cultural revival was underway.

Restoring the manor from the brutal troop occupation in the First World War had been hard—cupboards had been used as privies, banisters had been broken up and burnt as firewood, and the floors destroyed by heavy boots. During the latter part of the Second World War, the house was occupied again, and again virtually ruined, and it was only partially renovated in the Soviet era. After collectivisation in 1949, parts of it housed the collective farm office, until the new administrative block was built nearby. Then the manor house was locked up, and left to deteriorate.

Even that first day, as I walked around waiting for the key, I could see that there was something slightly odd about the spatial relationship between the culture hall, the school, the new blocks of flats, and the old manor house. All the modern buildings were placed in relation to one another: the school stood at a right angle to the culture hall, as did the blocks of flats, which also formed smaller squares amongst themselves. The manor house, on the other hand, stood at an indeterminate and slightly worrying angle to the rest. I eventually realised that what looked like the front of the manor— what had in effect become the front—must originally have been the back. The old drive was still just discernible. The front had fallen into disuse, since all the new blocks of flats were built on the fields behind it, and the house had swivelled on its axis. Facing the old front were a few acres of forgotten parkland, now overgrown and irrelevant. It was under renovation during my year in the village, a renovation that was to prove slow and fitful as the village ran out of money, but the old front was destined to remain the back.

It was mid-August, and yet it felt like autumn. The leaves were red and yellow, and it was already cold. That first evening I walked through the old village of Österby, and on to the sea. There was a smell of apples in the air, and something harsh and eastern European; I didn't then know what it was. A woman in a shawl was cutting wood on an ancient electrical saw, and two boys were fencing with sticks next to her. A roe deer jumped into the woods, and a crackly radio somewhere played a piece of classical music. On the way home I met a young woman with a child and an older couple. The man swayed towards me, arms slightly open, saying something quickly that I didn't understand. He stood near me, smiling, not very tall, blond, blue eyed, a bit washed out. Drunk. The older woman smiled; the younger one looked at me indifferently. I smiled cautiously and walked on.

It was cold in the visitors' flat. Now, twenty years later, I remember the cold, the narrow bed in my room, the dirt. The cold and dirt were equally haunting; I shrank into myself. I was there alone. Then, my obsessive mantra—*Now is the time for all good men to come to the aid of the party*—playing in my head, I heated water on the stove, and cleaned the room. Gripped by a sense of repulsion, I also cleaned the communal kitchen, the bathroom, and the corridor. The flat had four bedrooms along a wide corridor. It was pleasantly spacious, but dirty. There were hundreds, perhaps thousands, of dead flies in the corridor. I swept them all up, and threw them out of the window. I cooked porridge in an aluminium pan for supper, and later heated water in the same saucepan for tea and for washing.

There was no hot water and no heating. I remember the contrast between the Soviet rooms and the western cleaning materials I had brought—a harsh mix. The flat had for so long been cleaned with only cold water, with the black old rag still stored under the sink, that the scent of the new cleaning fluids felt overwhelming and wrong, a strange culture clash.

Earlier I had bought some supplies from the shop. In careful Estonian, I asked for milk. The woman behind the counter lifted up a steel bucket from under the counter. She took an empty beer bottle from a crate, rinsed it in cold water, and, with the help of a scoop and a metal cylinder, filled it with milk. With an impassive face, she handed me the bottle. Three people, eating vanilla ice cream, watched me in silence. I smiled, more uncertainly than I would have wished, and left.

I soon learnt that the harsh pollution in the village was from the brown coal. The coal, imported from Poland, was burnt in the rusty old furnace by the workshops. It left a faint yellow cloud hovering over the square, and an acrid taste in the mouth. As it turned out, the cloud of pollution wouldn't last long: the furnace broke down shortly after my arrival, and in any event there was no more subsidised Polish coal. After that, there was only intermittent heating, and a little lukewarm water once a week or so, for the rest of the year.

There was a Peace Corps volunteer in the village, Leigh, from Birmingham, Alabama. I think she may have been a nurse originally, but I am not sure about that. I do remember her aspiration: she wanted to be a massage therapist in Boulder, Colorado. She was enigmatic and heavy, with straight dark hair and green slightly slanted eyes. When I arrived in August she was still away, but I had met her before, during my first visit in the spring. She was there to teach English, to show the Estonian English teachers "new methods," and to disseminate cheerful Peace Corps materials to replace the (equally cheerful, and actually not altogether dissimilar) old Soviet schoolbooks.

On my first visit, she had taken me on a tour, showing me the tiny private cooperative shop, at that time still only a primitive kiosk, selling tinned food, cigarettes, chocolate, and shampoo. Two small brown fish flapped about on an orange plastic plate on the counter. She showed me the culture hall and the English schoolroom, which she had decorated with American posters. There was a photograph of Maryland in snow, captioned, "*The snow came down last night like moths / Burned on the moon; it fell till dawn, / Covered the town with simple cloths*"; a sunrise in a national park in Virginia titled, ". . . comes again. The welcome morning with its rays of peace"; and New York skyscrapers, with "*Lay me on an anvil, O God . . . Let me be the great nail holding a skyscraper through blue nights into white stars.*" The contrast with the flat, prosaic landscape outside could hardly have been greater.

Of course this was only four years after the end of the cold war. As we were walking Leigh told me that the energetic and intellectual young history teacher, Ivar, whom I had yet to meet, had uncharacteristically gotten drunk one evening and revealed that he was anti-American. I was not surprised. Laine, the blond and sophisticated headmistress, looking at me knowingly, European to European, had already intimated how nice it would be to have somebody teaching "English English" rather than "American English."

The third occupant of the communal flat that year was Timo, a young teacher who had exchanged compulsory military service for a stint of teaching in this remote region—it was almost impossible to attract young teachers to the area.

Leigh made dinner for us the first evening we were all together, a pizza cobbled together from what she could find. Timo kept lapsing into silence, staring out the window, bewildered and depressed at finding himself committed to teaching for a year in this primitive place. I cautiously began the process of participant observation with him, whilst he, I soon found out, really only wanted to talk about the contemporary European music scene—in that sense, we were a disappointment to each other.

Leigh talked, in a heavy southern drawl that lent drama and interest to her discourse, about how many Peace Corps volunteers had left Estonia because they had felt so discouraged and alone, in contrast to the pampered volunteers in Russia, Latvia, and Lithuania. Estonians didn't engage with the volunteers, she said, and any attempt on their part to get to know people failed miserably. Her students had told her that unless you have a specific reason to do so, it's *contrived* to smile at people you meet on the street. She said, also, that she had cried almost every day the previous year, and had been politely ignored most of the time. A volunteer friend on another remote collective farm who had assumed that his Estonian colleagues disliked him, after a solitary year of no invitations and little conversation, was surprised to find two of the women teachers in tears on the day he left, in desperation, to teach in Tallinn instead. When he asked why they were crying, they told him that they had "gotten used to him" by now. Leigh smiled her joyless smile. Timo sighed and stared out the now-dark window. I thought of the prospective informants in the shop, watching me in silence as I carefully asked for milk. Our first evening together was over.

Two

Former Owners

My first trip to Estonia was two years earlier, in the summer of 1991. The streets were dusty in Tallinn that summer, the weather warm. I remember the anxiety of accidentally swallowing glass from a Soviet bottle of mineral water crumbling in my mouth, and the ubiquitous smell of wood smoke and brown coal, even in the heat. I remember wooden houses with flaking paint, quiet streets, shoddy high-rise areas, people waiting in flimsy bus shelters. I remember the silence, and the cats watching the flocks of pigeons lifting from the walls of the old city. People were waiting, it seemed, to see what would happen next.

My father had an Estonian secretary, Lydia Saarman, one of the many Estonian refugees in Sweden. She had put me in touch with a childhood friend, Veevi Kirschbaum. Veevi, a small, stout woman in her sixties, with wide-set blue eyes and a determined manner, came to meet me at my hotel. We walked back to her nearby flat, full of books and knickknacks, a gilded mirror, a polished table, and framed photographs. I had asked Lydia what to bring her, and she said that it was difficult, in fact I think almost impossible, to find coffee at that time, so I brought her some as a gift. Veevi took it into the little kitchen and was gone for a long time. Later I realised that she had no filter papers, and had to boil the coffee and let it settle. She gave me heavy, greasy cake, which I ate hungrily, and said to me sternly, "But first of all, now, my darling, I speak to you quite seriously: tomorrow you go and you have breakfast! And you ask them what time they have dinner!"

Veevi, then retired, had been in charge of supervising the production of goods for export: peat to Austria, Italy, and Belgium; briquettes to Finland; seat belts to Poland, which were tested in Prague and Paris; concert pianos, ski boots, bicycle helmets, and gardening tools for "capitalist states" like England. She found a tiny battered notebook recording the goods, and read to me from it, translating into English, which she spoke well, from the Estonian. She made the "export plan" for fourteen factories. Her superior at the Ministry of Production was Jewish, she said, "a Jew from Kiev, a very intelligent man like all Jews."

She herself was not Jewish, and I don't think that her husband was either, though he may have been. He had died of heart failure many years ago. His name, Kirschbaum, was the kind of German-sounding name that many Estonians took in the nineteenth century. Despite her position, she was not a communist. She had lost too much, but also the weakness of central targets and plans had been obvious to everyone for a long time.

"Why do you think we have such thick paper in the Soviet Union?" she said. "Central office in Moscow demanded that a certain factory produced a certain amount in tons, and so it was easier to produce heavier paper than to produce more paper!" The same was true for tins: the tin factories had targets of weight, which meant that the tins became absurdly heavy. The machine weights, too, she said, were about ten times their weight from those in the West: "Everything was very heavy!"

Despite those failures, and there were many, there was a constant emphasis on technological achievements and progress in the Soviet Union. By 1991 that particular form of modernity only remained in dusty Soviet tourist books sold in the provinces. I bought and read them compulsively: "It would be no exaggeration to say that Tallinn produced everything from industrial equipment to sewing needles. 40% of the gross output of the republic is produced by Tallinn's industries, which export their goods to 86 foreign countries." "Goods are constantly being carried to and fro from Latvia, Lithuania, Leningrad and Kaliningrad." What the Soviets aspired to—the bustle of modernity, constant building ("Her architects are constantly designing new projects and the building never comes to a halt in the city"), endless work projects, import, export, industry of all kinds—they never quite achieved, and what we aspire to, or at least what I aspired to—peace and quiet—they had in abundance. It was so quiet, so peaceful, so beguilingly old-fashioned. Going to Estonia felt like travelling back in time, but the similarities between their present and our past were incidental and deceptive, hiding the years of Soviet repression and modernity: the collectivisation and "rationalisation" of agriculture, and the heavy postwar industrialisation in the eastern part of the country.

After coffee, Veevi showed me her photo albums. There was her husband, dark and good-looking, and her wartime friends. "This was my dear friend. She went to Siberia. And this is the picture she sent back." There was a stamp-sized photograph stuck under the larger pre-war picture of a sturdy girl with glossy waved hair. The girl in the Siberian picture had poorer clothes and flat hair, a hesitant smile in a thin face.

"And did she come back?" I asked.

"Yes. Oh yes. But her father was shot."

Woman survivors of Stalinism, Veevi told me, now spoke on the radio, in a series entitled *Unwritten Memories*. They described people dying from diarrhea after eating rotting scraps of food, and labour camps around electricity stations, built by prisoners. Male prisoners worked for an average of three months before they died. Then more people were arrested. "So was the communist empire built," she said.

Veevi and her late husband were "former owners," and she was now reclaiming the building they had owned in the independence era, a 1930s block of flats with a bakery on the ground floor. In 1950 the Red Army had demobilised, and many flats in Tallinn were confiscated and given to veterans. Veevi and her husband lost their building, and their own flat, and spent the next sixteen years in a room of nine square meters. They hid the deeds to the building in a tin, which they buried in the ground. They didn't dare to request a bigger flat, because it might remind the authorities of their status as "former owners." She had no children, but Veevi never gave up hope that the building would one day belong to her again, and that independence would be restored to Estonia. She took me to see it the next day.

"You understand, Sigrid," she said, fixing me with her blue eyes, "in Estonia we say, 'My home is my castle.'"

I took a photo of her outside it, a small and determined figure in front of the 1930s white block, legs apart, chin up, thick glasses resting on her broad nose.

Like many Estonians, Veevi kept her political allegiance to liberal Britain, the formerly secret voice of the BBC World Service, after independence. Voice of America, she thought, was not as good. I felt then that the reality of contemporary Britain, and the West, was almost certain to disappoint her, and I think eventually it did. Veevi, at heart, was an idealist. She believed in freedom, and in high culture, and she was puzzled and dismayed by our cultural relativism, our consumerism, and our lack of ideals.

When I left later that week, she came with me in my rented car to the airport. We almost got lost, but then we saw the new Swedish Statoil petrol station by the airport. I returned the car, which took an inordinately long time. A gentle young woman puzzled over the rental form for at least half an hour, and when she deemed her detailed scrutiny of each entry to have been completed, she smiled shyly, and gave me a box. I was, it turned out, their first customer, and this was my present: a pale plastic doll with white hair dressed in an Estonian national costume. Veevi told me her name was Maja.

I came back in November 1991, a few months after the coup in Russia, and the Estonian parliament's *Resolution on Immediate Independence*, which had made Estonia an independent country. This time I travelled to Tallinn on the overnight ferry run by Estline. Dizzy from a sleepless and nauseous night, I waited in the long queue to get through passport control. There were Swedish entrepreneurs (all men), some day-trippers, and many mysterious and rough men with pale faces, dirty jeans, and long, greasy hair. The Hotel Viru, where I was staying, was a collection point for the latter group. They hung out with the prostitutes and illegal currency dealers on the second floor, the sun falling through plate-glass windows onto blue clouds of smoke. Viru was the downmarket hotel for Westerners. There were several cheaper hotels for Easterners, and then there was the upmarket Western-style Hotel Palace.

The Red Army was still occupying the military bases then, and there were Soviet soldiers on the streets. Street signs were bilingual, and Russians in public jobs were not yet required to speak Estonian. One night I went to a concert of Beethoven and Mozart at the newly restored concert house performed by the Eesti Riiklik Sümfooniaorkester. The music was soothing; the concert house was beautiful, and as I listened I felt increasingly at home. At the intermission, however, when the entire audience formed itself into a silent train of people, tramping slowly round and round in a circle, neatly turning by the stairs, Estonia once again felt like a foreign country. I didn't join it. I looked, instead, at the framed photographs of conductors and musicians on the wall, and the ominous dates: Eduard Oja (1905–50), Evald Aav (1900–39), Adolf Vedro (1890–1944).

After the concert I walked back to the hotel through the rain. The streets were flooded and people hurried by with small and colourful umbrellas. There were few cars, I assumed because of the current petrol crisis. I had dinner in the hotel for 15 roubles, then about 15 pence. A young couple tried to exchange money with me—they would give me 55 roubles, not one or two, for a dollar, they said. They looked so Western that at first I took them for tourists trying to change dollars for roubles, but of course they were not. On the way back to my room I stopped to buy a bottle of mineral water in the bar, which turned out to be hard currency only. Thus my dinner cost 15 pence, and my bottle of sparkling water—not Western, I might add—cost a pound. Such was the currency discrepancy in 1991. The following summer, in 1992, the Estonian kroon was reintroduced, and the exchange rate was set at 10 roubles per kroon. People could exchange a maximum of 1,500 roubles. If you had, say, 1,000 roubles in your bank account, a reasonable sum by old Soviet standards, you could change it for 100 kroon, which in turn was worth about a dollar and a half.

There were two middle-aged Swedish men in that bar. One of them, heavy and plain, was talking to a glamorous young woman. The two men glared at each other, competing, perhaps, over the woman. They ordered drinks, and the barman stirred them with a studied pre-war flourish. The woman looked at me and smiled into her drink, a moment of complicity between us. None of us—the bartender, the prostitute, the men, or I—knew quite how to act in this new situation. The portals were opening to alternative futures, and closing to the past.

At 10:30 that night I had a crackly conversation with Veevi. She had made me promise to ring her before going to bed, because she was worried about the new criminality in Tallinn. There were one or two murders a week, she said, and rapes and muggings. There were gangs from Russian and the Caucasus. "They talk about the blue-eyed Estonians," she said, the naive Estonians they can mug and rob. "So, my darling, you must promise me, promise me when you come back from the concert that you ring me, anytime. First you must eat. Then you ring me." I tried, also, to call a friend in Sweden, but the number for the international operator was "unavailable." I plugged in the TV instead, and jumped back as sparks flew from the socket. Then I saw the disconnected wire, copper threads brittle and torn hanging uselessly from the back, and gave up.

A friend in England had put me in touch with someone he knew in Tallinn: Riina, a journalist and TV reporter. I met her at her office.

"Can you recognise the Russians on the street?" I asked her, thinking of my conversations with Veevi about Russian criminality.

"Yes, I think so," she said. "I think I do. But you see, my grandmother was Russian. So I could never be a right-wing radical nationalist."

Her Estonian grandmother, she then said, had been a friend of the war criminal Ain-Ervin Mere. He ran a concentration camp for the Germans. After the war he escaped to England under a death sentence. Mere, I found out later, was an *obersturmbannführer* in the Waffen SS, and the head of the Nazi Estonian security police, the *Sicherheitspolizei*, created in 1942. In 1961 he was condemned to death in the first Soviet Holocaust trials. The British authorities, however, did not extradite him, and he died in Leicester, aged sixty-six.

The 1961 Soviet trial charged Estonian collaborators with the murder of Jews and gypsies, focusing on atrocities near Kalevi-Liiva, the killing fields of the Jägala concentration camp in 1942–43. The trial was held in the auditorium of the Naval Officers Club in Tallinn. All four defendants were found guilty. Two of them, Ralf Gerrets, deputy commandant at the Jägala camp, and Jaan Viik, a guard at the camp, were convicted and executed. Viik was accused of throwing small children into the air and shooting them, a charge he did not deny. Camp Commandant Aleksander Laak was eventually found in Canada, and subsequently committed suicide.

Ain-Ervin Mere was also tried, and convicted in absentia. He had overseen the selection process of the Jews, who had been transported to Estonia from Berlin and the concentration camp Theresienstadt outside Prague. Once in Estonia, some of the men were selected for slave labour at the oil shale mines, and a very few of the women were sent for other slave labour work. A handful of women, having been sent around various camps, were eventually liberated at Bergen-Belsen. The majority, including all the elderly and all the children, were murdered. Most were shot, either by police or by camp guards.

There were further trials after that, and two other perpetrators were found: Ervin Viks, who had fled to Australia, and Karl Linnas, who had escaped to the United States. They were accused of taking part in the murder of twelve thousand Jews in the Tartu concentration camp. Australia and the United States refused extradition, Australia citing the lack of extradition treaties with the Soviet Union. Viks died, a free man, in Australia in 1983. Linnas was in fact eventually extradited from the United States in 1986, and died in a Soviet prison.

The Holocaust was horrific in Estonia. And no one that I met ever talked about it.

Later that evening, I tried ringing Ain Sarv, the editor of the contemporary Swedish Estonian magazine *Ronor*, based on the west coast. It was a very bad line. At that time local lines worked reasonably well, but the telephone lines across the country barely functioned. I heard, finally, a weak voice say, "Hallo?"

"Hallo," I said in Swedish. "Do you speak Swedish?"

She immediately hung up.

I had dinner with some Finnish aid workers at the hotel that night. They said they had heard that the Russian troops were leaving. You still saw them around town: young men, almost boys, in long grey coats, and their hats with the red star—hats you could already buy as souvenirs in Berlin. They were gradually leaving, though the last troops stayed until 1994.

The next morning I went to the travel bureau in the hotel to ask about trains to Haapsalu, the main town of western Estonia. A crowd of unfriendly and irritable people was pressing forward. The room was a fug of cigarette smoke. When I finally got to the desk, the woman escorted me into another room, where I was met by friendly and helpful people, who said that they could organise everything. This was the Western currency zone.

Haapsalu was the nearest town to my prospective field site. It had been a spick-and-span little coastal town in the 1930s, a summer spa where people came for the mineral mud baths. Now, the baths were long since gone, the paint on the beautiful wooden houses flaking and unkempt. There were broken windows everywhere and, strikingly, piles and piles of firewood, even outside the modern buildings. These were mostly grey concrete blocks, cracked and unpainted. The main street was wide and muddy, with many shops selling few things, and almost no cars. It was intensely cold.

I had gone by slow train from Tallinn, waved on by chubby women stationmasters at each little country station. My first sight of Haapsalu was a film scene, set in the nineteenth century. The film team, scruffy men in black caps, cheap cigarettes in mouths, themselves looked like actors in a Soviet film. They had been waiting for our train, which they now obscured with clouds of smoke, to look like a steam train. Over the flaking Estonian exit sign they had hung a new one, in German: AUSGANG. The camera rolled, and the actors exited, one by one.

Two years later I saw another film on a Tallinn street. This scene was of the Soviet era, with a shop window laid out exactly as I remembered them: a few artfully arranged cans of fish, and not much more. Fake snow on the ground. All the actors and members of the film crew must have remembered what those windows were like, with their handwritten signs: PIIMA EI OLE. "No milk." Or "No meat." Every language in the Soviet Union had a standard expression for "not available"; *ei ole* was the Estonian one. The very recent past seemed so long ago then, with Estonia saturated not only with 1970s cast-offs from the West, but also with all the new and techy markers of the future: mobile phones, laptops, shiny petrol stations with supermarkets, glossy food packaging and soft drinks—all so hard and shiny in the still grey post-Soviet world.

In Haapsalu, that cold November day in 1991, schoolchildren in woolly hats and mittens went by, eating vanilla ice cream. Everybody hurried on. I tried to talk to many of them, to see if I could find any Estonian Swedish contacts. After many unsuccessful encounters, I eventually found someone who was willing to talk and who was, also, married to an Estonian Swede. "There are not many Swedes left in Estonia now," she said, "and the children have all become Estonian." She smiled, revealing uneven brown teeth.

I eventually took the bus back to Tallinn, an impossibly crowded and very warm bus, that stopped at every village en route. A young woman, a self-appointed minder, walked with me from the tram to the hotel, so that I wouldn't lose my way. I thanked her profusely, and she nodded, smiled a secret smile, and melted back into the streets. In the hotel, I booked a flight back to Stockholm before ringing Veevi, as I had promised. I knew by then that she thought my capacity for planning was feeble, at best, so I expected a thorough conversation about logistics.

"Now, Sigrid," she began firmly. "Did you get your ticket already?"

"No, but I booked it," I said, feeling confident that my booking was solid, and that that might be the end of the matter. I had, after all, travelled widely across most continents, booking my own flights since I was seventeen.

"You booked it," she said thoughtfully. "And when will you get it?"

"The day I fly, at the airport."

"At the airport. They told you this?"

"Yes," I said patiently. "I spoke to the airline office, and they took my booking."

"They took your booking. Did they take your name?"

"Yes."

"They took your family name?"

"Yes."

"But then, Sigrid, I have such a feeling that you will have to be at the airport earlier to get your ticket."

"Yes, they told me I should be there by 2:40. The plane doesn't depart until 6:25."

"Ah," she said heavily. "Well, I am sorry for asking all these questions, but you see, to do anything here you have to control every step."

That evening she introduced me to Matti Päts, the grandson of the former president, Konstantin Päts. We travelled by tram to Mustamäe, the high-rise suburb of Tallinn, where he lived. Matti, a tall, heavily built man in his sixties, with blue eyes and cropped hair, opened the door. His wife hovered behind him, smiling nervously. Unlike Matti, she didn't speak English.

In 1940, following the Soviet annexation of Estonia, Konstantin Päts and his whole family were arrested. Matti's uncle managed to escape to Sweden, but the rest of them were deported. Matti was seven years old. They were sent, he said, in the grand state Wagon Lit from Estonia to Moscow, and on from Moscow in normal trains. His mother was imprisoned in a camp near Sverdlovsk (now Yekaterinburg). His father was deported to another camp, where he died. Matti and his brother were incarcerated in a camp for children of the deported near the Ural Mountains. There, the guards indoctrinated them in "Marxist-Leninist and Stalinist thought." Konstantin Päts, they learnt, was a "traitor to the working people of Estonia." The townspeople sometimes threw bread or potatoes over the fence. They could see that the children were hungry, and suspected, rightly, that the guards stole their rations. "My friends who have not been there," he said, "they cannot imagine what it is like to be hungry. To be weak. To have nothing." His brother, weaker than him, starved to death in that camp, officially described as an "orphanage."

He showed me a photograph of himself taken by the town photographer just before he was freed in 1946. He was twelve then, a thin boy with a shaved head, dressed in an old uniform, much too big for him. His mother was liberated in the same year, and the two of them returned to Estonia. He hadn't been allowed to speak Estonian in the orphanage, so he could hardly remember his own language. In 1950 his mother was deported again, as a "socially dangerous person." This time she did not survive, and Matti was on his own.

President Päts died in 1956 in a special mental hospital in the Kalinin (now Tver) oblast. On 21 October 1990 he was given a state funeral in Tallinn. The streets were packed, and Prime Minister Edgar Savisaar made a speech. Matti also spoke, numb with cold, but warmed up, he said, by the television lights. The uncle who fled to Sweden settled outside Arlöv, a small town in the south, where he worked as a gardener. Matti tried to contact him when he was first allowed to visit Stockholm, but with no success. "He was paralysed with fear," he said.

The Päts family gave us dinner that evening: boiled sausage, cold carrots and peas mixed in a white sauce, with side dishes of potatoes and pumpkin. They grew their own vegetables in a small plot. Veevi, sipping the sweet white wine, was becoming increasingly animated and determined, "like the Queen of England," Matti said teasingly. "I knew her husband very well, and when she would get that manner we used to tell her she was acting like the Queen of England." Veevi laughed, and even Matti's wife smiled.

She smiled and nodded to me, and I smiled and nodded back. Then she brought out the photo albums. I politely looked through album after album, until I finally asked them about the failed communist coup in Russia, which had taken place less than three months before I arrived, 19–21 August 1991. President Gorbachev had been kept a prisoner at his dacha by the KGB, and the lines of communication to Moscow cut. The putsch did not succeed, but it might have, in which case the Soviet Union, in perhaps a slightly different form, would have survived. What had it been like in Estonia? "Well," said Matti. "I was in Helsinki at the time. I was not going to go back. I was not going to live through it once more."

Veevi, she said, had gone out to the telephone tower where people gathered in response to Prime Minister Savisaar's call for help on the radio. The telephone tower was the centre of communications, and hundreds of unarmed people gathered there to defend it against the coming Russian tanks. The radio solemnly announced the progress of the tanks: 200 kilometers from Tallinn; 175 kilometers from Tallinn; 150 kilometers from Tallinn . . . The people built barricades and stood in groups, waiting. Veevi was with a group of women. At about three in the morning, she said, a young Estonian, "a man of the people, a blue-eyed man with such an open, honest face, came up to us and said: 'Women of Estonia! Go home and protect our homes! Protect yourselves so that the Estonian people may survive!'" She went home, then, but continued to listen to the radio. Savisaar called again on the men of Estonia to come out to the telephone tower, and soon afterwards she heard cars hooting everywhere—the people who had cars were offering lifts to those who didn't. The summer night turned to dawn, and the tanks, halted outside Tallinn, never arrived. The Russian coup failed, and three days later, on 24 August 1991, Russia officially recognised the independence of Estonia. On 6 September the Soviet Union, officially still in existence, did too.

*   *   *

Before I left Tallinn that November, Veevi and a friend of hers took me for a drive. We drove to the Summer Palace in her friend's rattling old car, and on to the Forest Cemetery, and the Song Festival Amphitheatre. We walked around the cemetery and talked about what people were like when they came back from the camps. Were they broken by their experiences? "No! You see, Sigrid, the best people were deported, and the ones who were hopeful survived. The pessimists all died."

We went on to a mostly Russian high-rise area. The houses were badly built and cracking, and the road too strangely wide to lead anywhere except back. We stopped by the sea. There was a cold wind, and the water was as grey as the sky. The restaurant where we parked the car was empty. November, as everyone had told me, was indeed the low season in this most seasonal of countries.

THREE

The Russians

It was spring 1993 before I saw Veevi again. She invited me for dinner in her flat. We talked whilst she cooked, a documentary about Israeli wildlife running quietly on the Finnish channel to which the TV was tuned. She gave me boiled potatoes with a little meat, pickled cucumbers and sour Georgian white wine, and *pasha*: a little triangle of creamy pudding with a pink plastic rose planted on top.

"These cups are very beautiful," I said, holding a cup of coffee.

"Oh yes, that is Rosenthal. That is not the only Rosenthal I have."

"Is it from before the war?" I asked politely.

"Oh yes, and everything—this!"—she gesticulated energetically at the curved dark wood sideboard—"this!"—a glass cabinet—"this!" She stepped towards the old desk, and accidentally knocked the thermos on the floor. There were coffee grounds everywhere, because there were still no filter papers. She ineffectually scraped the stain on the oriental carpet, and then swept up the wet grounds.

By now she had claimed back her building. Independent Estonia had passed a law allowing former owners to reclaim properties that had been confiscated by the Soviet state. If you didn't demand compensation for the loss of value due to wear and tear, the claim was processed quicker, and hers was one of the first. She was about to get it back, and wanted to sell it, preferably for hard currency, but she didn't know how. There were no Estonian estate agents yet. She had no access to, or concept of, the market, which was gradually developing. "Contacts! I need contacts! When I was working I had plenty!" she said with frustration. She couldn't conceive of the idea that the building was only worth as much as anyone was willing to pay for it, and I think, also, that she was right to mistrust the market. But neither did she have any idea what the intrinsic worth of the property might be, nor did anyone else. There was a new law governing appropriate house prices, designed to curb speculation, and a civil servant had to approve the price. Her first attempt to sell, indeed, had not been passed by the official, who had deemed the price too low.

In the middle of an intense speech about the legal develop-ments, her hands clenched, I felt a sudden need of distraction, so I interrupted her: "Veevi, would you mind if I had a cigarette," I asked, "or don't you like the smoke?"

"For forty years," she said, "for forty years I smoked. That is why I am now so fat." In one energetic movement she got up, opened a cupboard in the bookcase, and brought out a new pack of ciga-rettes and an ashtray. "You know, when a person stops smoking it is a tragedy."

Then she gave me the recipe for the *pasha*:

1 kilogram quark (milk curd)
100 grams butter
1.5 cups sugar
200 grams sour cream
250 millilitres whipping cream
3 egg yolks
more than 50 grams orange rind preserve
more than 50 grams nuts or almonds
tiny bit of salt

"Take quark and sieve it," she said. "The sense is that the quark must be very, very tiny. Clean the nuts. You take a pot and the first thing this one hundred grams butter in the pot. Everything in *kastrul* [saucepan] and you make mishmash. The first thing you melt the butter. Then almost boil everything. Don't boil. Don't let it boil. Ninety-nine degrees. Then cool. Form it like pyramid and press it with . . . what do you call it? Cloth—thin cloth. In the fridge for twelve hours. This is Russian Easter dish."

At her prompting, I wrote down the recipe, and then sat peacefully smoking her cigarettes as she continued talking about the new economy, about the directors of state enterprises who created private marketing companies to channel goods into the shops, making a 300 percent profit. Managing directors "solved" the problems of debt-ridden companies by selling machinery cheaply and quickly to companies, consortiums of which they were co-owners. Four out of five new banks had gone bankrupt. There were moratoriums on most important developments, and the economy was corroded by significant corruption. She ended, emphatically: "The new economy is shivering on his legs."

She also talked about the Mafia, their extortionate demands for protection money, and the beatings, explosions, and attacks when protection money was not paid. In those days you saw the Mafia guys on the road, in their black Mercedes-Benzes, black leather jackets and very short hair. They come, she said, from the "wild Caucasus," because "the border is not in order." I asked whether Estonians, too, were involved in crime. "The rackets—are they Estonian, are they Russian? Who knows?" She looked away. "A *masculino* can answer you—criminality is not women's domain. These," she said precisely, smiling her special smile, part irony, part sweet child, "are the infant illnesses of democracy. Eat your *pasha*! Frightful calories!"

Later, at dusk, I walked back to the Hotel Viru. Two men were on the street, tall and dark, dressed in black leather jackets and dark trousers. They walked slowly down the street, past an apartment building. One of them tried the door, whilst the other looked back. It was locked. They walked on, casually trying the door of a car farther on. It also was locked. I stopped to look at them, and they stopped, too, looking back at me. No one else was on the street. I was not afraid at the time. If anything I was amused by this living illustration of Veevi's prejudices, but I now think that perhaps I should have been at least a little wary.

In 1993 about a third of the total population of Estonia was Russian, a large and deliberate increase since the war and the Soviet invasion. Russian workers came to work in the new heavy industry, most of it located in eastern Estonia. Of all the former Soviet nations except Russia itself, only Kazakhstan and Latvia had a higher percentage of Russians. In 1939 the proportion of Estonians in Estonia had been 92 percent; by 1988 that figure had declined to 61 percent. The total population before the war had been 1,136,000 people; by 1945 it was 854,000. The demographic data made bleak reading for the Estonians.

The history of the Russians in Estonia was that of a ruling class, of imperialist colonisers. But still, in the Estonian discourse about them there were chilling echoes of other racist discourses. The "Russians," objectified by the Estonians, reminded me of the "natives" of the colonial imagination: happy-go-lucky, hospitable people lacking industry, application, and predictability. They were said to be a lumpen proletariat. They would go anywhere. They were drifters, people said, "metastases of the KGB." They let themselves down, drinking and wasting time. After the Soviet takeover in 1940, and, even more so, in the second occupation of 1944, the state of Russia itself became clear from the behaviour of the occupying Russian soldiers. They were informed, and apparently believed, that the food in the Estonian shop windows was Potemkin food, made out of plaster, a bourgeois deception. They had never seen flushing lavatories. The wives who came later mistook the nightgowns in the shops for ball gowns. And so on and so on. The stories about the Russians were the same all over newly occupied Europe. "You must feel pitiness for them," said Veevi airily.

Later in the year I set an essay question for my seventeen-year-old students entitled "Estonia: East or West?" These are some extracts: ·

I think it's natural, that if I live in some other country I must to learn that country's language. And also would be good to know that country's costumes [sic]. Just for that Estonians hate Russians, because they don't want to testify that they live in Estonia. They are trying to have power also here—they are expecting that we surrender to them.

My grandmother is Ukrainian. Once when she was in the company of her Russian friends who doesn't speak Estonian at all (but have lived here more than my granny) and when they noticed that my granny spoke Estonian, they said that she was a traitor.

We thought that we can't live without Russia, because it was so big and powerful. We had a beautiful red flag with sickle and hammer and were proud of it. I remember when I became a pioneer, I was so happy and when I went home, I got many flowers and then we (I mean my mother and I) went to restaurant "Moscow." And the pioneer necktie was so beautiful, and we were so sad when Leonid Breznev [sic] died. Then we couldn't even imagine that Estonia could be an independent state. But it happened, and I think that we did the right thing. At least we are not east anymore, though our life is not very easy. Look, what happens in Russia? There are all kind of problems: a rouble is not money anymore, they have terrible diseases and political crisis etc. I read that Russia is a prison for nations.

But anyway, minorities are and will be strangers, no matter if they speak or don't speak Estonian, if they want or don't want to become a citizen of Estonia. I hope so much that after ten years comes a day when in Estonia shines sun and people are happy. But now we are like "republic of bananas"—Estonia is "republic of patatios" [*sic*]. It is only my opinion.

In order to qualify for automatic Estonian citizenship, Russians had to prove that they had moved to the country before the first Soviet occupation, in 1940. If they had come later, which the majority had, they could still apply for citizenship. There was a language test for this group, requiring a vocabulary of some fifteen hundred words. Many Estonians complained that the Russians hadn't bothered to learn Estonian during the years of occupation, but in my experience if Russians tried to speak Estonian they were usually answered in Russian. Estonian only developed a print culture beyond Bible translations in the nineteenth century. It had for so long been a very private language. The Baltic German landowners spoke German, and the language of government was Russian. Estonians who managed to move from serfdom or peasant poverty to trade spoke German, and often Germanised their names.

After the Soviet occupation, few Estonians actually expected, or possibly even wanted, the Russians who settled in Estonia to learn the language. Do you want the occupier to speak your language? Probably not, I think.

"Many of them lived here for forty years, you know," Veevi said, smiling her disarming smile, "and they never bothered to learn our language. Now they say it is such a human rights question when we ask them to know fifteen hundred words. And the international commissions have been here and they understand very well what is our situation." And then she told me a terrible joke about the Russian who was horrified when he found out that he would have to learn fifteen hundred Estonian words, since in Russian he only knew three hundred . . .

When Veevi relaxed after dinner, though, she would tell me about her travels east. There was a note of nostalgia and glamour about these stories. She had seen the ship *Eva Braun* moored on the Black Sea, which Germany had given the Soviet Union as part of the reparations after the war. For a small extra charge you could see Hitler's cabin. She talked about beautiful but dirty Georgia with its dangerous men, about ancient Armenia and Kazakhstan. In Armenia, at one time, she was sharing a room with a friend, and a dark man, almost naked, "covered with hair," tried to get into the room. "They are very passionate, you know, and very good-looking often, the men. The women . . . they age quickly. They become heavy." All those places had become dangerous and inaccessible then, the Soviet holiday resorts on the Black Sea gradually decaying.

I visited Veevi again after my first week on the collective farm. She took me to the Tallinn farmers' market, which was housed in an indoor hall. The market was a wonder of abundance and order: a variety of vegetables neatly stacked, shining red cranberries, many kinds of wild mushrooms in pleasant woven baskets, fish boxes decorated with small grey stonefish. Veevi, however, complained that the market was dirty, compared to what it had been before the war. She talked about how people don't care anymore and fight with each other all the time. The Russian vegetable vendor responded to her in Estonian, and she answered in Russian, smiling coldly.

She was a little distracted because of her real estate problem. She had learnt that she couldn't sell the house without the land on which it stood, and reclaiming land was a more complex process than reclaiming buildings. She had, also, found a potential buyer, a young man. Now she was anxious that the delay might lead him to "betray" her by walking away from the deal.

The atmosphere in Tallinn was tense after a bomb had destroyed the Estonian Air offices. There were rumours about corruption and political intrigue. People were divided about whether the criminal gangs would have planned such a large attack, bigger than anything they had done previously. Veevi invited me to stay the night at her flat rather than at a hotel, thinking it safer.

That evening she told me so many stories. She told me about Finnish president Kekkonen's unofficial visit to Estonia, in 1964. She was there on the streets with the growing silent crowds as his car sped through Tallinn. He spoke to the students at Tartu University so inspiringly, so movingly, she said, about not forgetting their national heroes. The bonds between Finland and Estonia, linguistic as well as geographical, are strong—the Finno-Ugric language group is very small, and much of the history between the two countries is shared.

She talked about the Prague Spring (1968), when foreigners first started to come to Estonia, accompanied, always, by people from Moscow, from the Ministry of Foreign Trade and the KGB. She told me about a trade fair in Vienna, and being interviewed by the KGB at the Hotel Palace before being given permission to go. At the fair she had seen a stand with curious-looking plastic helmets, and tried one on. "Don't do it, Kirschbaum," said a male colleague "You'll ruin your hair. Here, let me." He tried on the unusual helmet with the two vertical flaps, and at that moment the manager of the factory came in, and doubled up with laughter: the helmets were the latest model of detachable bidets for a new housing area where all the fittings were built to 75 percent normal size. "Then I would listen to my boss speaking on the phone, saying, 'That Kirschbaum! She is forcing the men to wear bidets as hats!'" She laughed until the tears were running down her cheeks.

That night I tossed and turned on her hard and narrow sofa, until she called to me from her bedroom: "Sigrid! You want a sleeping tablet?"

"Oh!" I said, unused to such things. "Well, yes, if you have one . . ." Earlier she had wanted to insert raw onion into my nose, and wrap my feet in cloth with a hot garlic mash, to cure my cold, and now I got a tiny Russian pill to put me to sleep. I took it, and seemed to instantly dream that I was looking into the rear view mirror of a moving car. The reflection was intricate, and strikingly beautiful, and I was watching with fascination, when the mirror suddenly cracked violently, exploding into a nonreflective surface, like rough brown paper. It was a curiously apt metaphor for my fieldwork.

FOUR

The New Reality

There were three roads out of the main village of the collective farm, two of them dirt roads. The paved road led to the church, and then out to the mainland through marshy lowlands. The second road led to the sea, past the only new houses in the village, one of which belonged to the mayor, and the other to the builder. The last road went south, past the dilapidated workshops, ending by a little harbour on a muddy beach. From there, in the distance, you could see Haapsalu, the nearest town.

Through September there were many visits by exiled Estonian Swedes and their families. They arrived in their Volvos—always Volvos—on the *Estonia* or its sister ship, and drove out to the peninsula. The farmhouses they had grown up in were usually more or less untouched since the war, in varying states of neglect and disrepair. Sometimes they were mended, or extended, with the ubiquitous white brick of Soviet Estonia; sometimes they were patched up with odd pieces of wood. There was always electricity, but rarely running water or sanitation.

The state of the people mirrored the state of the houses. The Swedes who had left as children had grown taller than their relatives who had stayed. They had their own teeth. They looked healthy and well, calm and confident. The ones who had stayed behind were stiff and bent, with bad teeth, raised on poor food, on caution and mistrust. Now, in old age, they had little medical or dental care, their bodies marked by "bad governance," that seemingly abstract concept, just as "good governance" was written on the bodies of the Swedes.

There was, in fact, only a handful of native Swedish speakers left on the peninsula, and none of them had much to do with the revival. But because the idea of revival dated back to the nineteenth century, because a flavour of Swedishness was still present in place names and historical memory, and because so much was at stake for the impoverished post-Soviet villagers, the absence of genuine Swedes didn't seem to matter much. Many people with one or more Swedish grandparent rediscovered roots. Swedish and Finnish goodwill, and the wish to help a neighbouring country, was part of it, too. The evacuated Estonian Swedes, with their families, helped as well, as did the local Swedish societies and schools. The logic of the Soviet cultural landscape, such as it was, had crumbled; the local hope of a special affiliation with Sweden, encouraged by entrepreneurs and cultural activists, replaced it.

The mayor and the headmistress of the school were at the forefront of building links to Sweden. The village school was divided between the first nine years, for local children, and the high school, formerly a Soviet language-oriented specialist school with boarding facilities. The two were quite distinct, though it was run as one school and reinvented as a "Swedish" school. The Swedish Council sent a Swedish teacher, as did the Finnish Council. (Swedish is an official language in Finland, and the Finnish Council also had an interest in the Swedes in Estonia.) All the teachers and members of the council went for Swedish language training in the Finnish twin town, the mainly Swedish-speaking Kronoby.

Laine Belovas, the headmistress of the school, was the wife of the former director of the collective farm, who had retired to run a garage in Haapsalu. They had obviously lost most of their authority with the demise of the collective farm, and rumours of corruption (mink coats, trips to Florida) clung to them. Laine, however, was navigating these difficulties with some skill. Probably about forty-five then, she was blond and handsome, and spoke Swedish well.

The Swedes who visited the school were always informally dressed. For them, the visit was a field trip to a remote, primitive, possibly even dangerous area, and they arrived dressed for it, in practical and warm clothes. Laine mimicked this informality, wearing clothes during these meetings that she would never wear during the course of an ordinary school day: jeans and sweaters, flat shoes, little or no make-up. Her blond hair, normally elaborately puffed up, was flat and natural. When the Swedes left she turned back to her usual Estonian persona: elegant dress, make-up, stockings and medium-heeled shoes. Dressing down was dressing up, in the world turned upside down.

In 1993 the future of the collective farm was still uncertain. The land and buildings had been taken over by a transitory privatisation commission. There was talk about turning it into a company, but it was unclear which parts might be involved, or how it could be done. People could potentially buy land, but to my knowledge no one had done so. "Former owners" could, and did, reclaim their farmhouses. Most of the farms had received several claims from Sweden, and there was talk of a new law coming into force ruling that only permanent residents would be able to get their property back. Some people feared that the farmhouses would turn into summer homes for the Swedes. That was hard to imagine in 1993, in that broken, dirt-poor community, where people were leaving every week on rickety Soviet lorries for some new future somewhere else.

Hard to imagine, also, why people would fear it. The Swedish revival, on the whole, gave hope to the people on the peninsula. In 1989 it had resumed as abruptly as it had ended in 1939. The son of the first headmaster of the Birkas school, Olle Söderbäck, was a member of the town council of the Swedish town Åtvidaberg. He initiated a twin town agreement between Pürksi and Åtvidaberg, which in effect had turned into an aid programme for the village. Thus Pürksi had become, again, a centre for Swedishness, despite the fact that there were actually only a handful of Estonian Swedes left on the peninsula. By the time I got there, there was already a facade of Swedishness in the village. Lorry-loads of furniture, and all kinds of equipment and machinery, had been shipped over. There was a new—and as far as I could tell completely unused—library, stocked with an eclectic assortment of Swedish second-hand books. There was a communal freezer, where people could rent compartments. There were regular shipments of clothes and other things, and charity sales for the villagers, the proceeds going to a fund to benefit the community.

The most important project in the village was a new woodchip heating system, which was completed towards the end of my stay, after a winter of virtually no communal heating, with outside temperatures dropping to minus 33 degrees centigrade. District heating was standard in the Soviet Union, and under-heating was rarely a problem. In the winter of 1993–94, however, on this collective farm, the heating was intermittent at best. The village authorities continued to issue bills—post-Soviet and therefore unsubsidised—for the nonexistent heat, which most of the villagers patiently paid. Even in September, the school was so cold. The children sat huddled in their coats. By deep winter they were wrapped up in scarves, woolly hats, and mittens, Swedish cast-offs, mostly. I wore, always, jeans, boots, a T-shirt, an old Armani jacket, and a calve-length woollen coat.

The post office had a Swedish post office sign. The private co-op shop in the village had Swedish supermarket posters in the window. Haapsalu, the local town, was full of Swedish advertising posters, often with endearingly tenuous relationships to the goods actually available. Several such posters, for instance, from a reputable and substantial Swedish outlet, confidently promised, in Swedish, "All you need for the heating systems of your home." Homemade arrows led to the shop itself, a small room, where a few obsolete Soviet electrical instruments were arranged on dusty shelves. I don't know where they got the posters—perhaps they wrote and asked for them. Like Soviet slogans and the now rusty old Soviet signs, the posters were about identity and ideology, not commerce or even the actual existence of goods for sale.

History was turning, and the historical process of the revolution was reversing itself. Boris Pasternak describes how Yuri in *Doctor Zhivago* found the remnants of prerevolutionary shop signs out in countryside. All advertising had long since disappeared in revolutionary Moscow:

> Living in Moscow, Yury had forgotten how many shop signs there still were in other towns and how much of the facades they covered. Some of those he was seeing now were so large that he could read them easily from where he stood, and they came down so low over the slanting windows of the sagging, one-storyed buildings that the crooked little houses were almost hidden by them, like the faces of village children in their fathers' peaked cap.

There is a poignancy to those signs of a lost world of solidity and enterprise:

> There were round red oil tanks in the field, and large advertisements on wooden billboards. One of them caught the doctor's eye twice. It bore the inscription: "Moreau & Vetchinkin. Mechanical seeders. Threshing machines." "That was a good firm. Their agricultural machinery was first-rate."

The advertising I found were signs from the imagined future, from "normal life," that sunny Western garden. My villagers were familiar with the concept. Many of them had visited Finland or Sweden, and knew that Soviet Estonia was "not normal," a state they hoped would be temporary as Estonia moved from the Soviet sphere to its rightful place in the northern European one. Most of the aid went to western and central Estonia. There was soon a style fault line between western and eastern Estonia—the east, where most of the Russians lived, remained Soviet in style, whilst the west and the centre quickly became Westernised.

After the first few weeks in the village, I slowly began to feel at home. I was also, in some sense, coming home to a culture and a landscape familiar from childhood. Virtually everybody in the village wore clothes donated from Sweden. I had grown up amongst those jeans and T-shirts and jackets and boots; they were part of my memories. I had left Sweden thirteen years before I came to the collective farm, and the donated clothes seemed to belong to my teenage years. I saw a woman in Sami boots—in 1970s Sweden those boots signalled prog music, vegetarianism, ecology, and anti-imperialism; here, depoliticised, they still spoke to me, in the mildly surreal and secret language of things. The fact that those clothes were old and second-hand masked their newness to me, but the villagers, too, wore them with nonchalance. For them there was no contradiction between the concepts of new and normal. As in Russia, "normal" meant good, or okay, but it was also the ubiquitous expression for what Estonia—one's life, one's flat, one's work—ought to become, rather than what it was. Estonia was still "not normal."

The peninsula was big—some thirty by fifty kilometers. About a third of the land was forest: the old forests and, nearer to the village, the newer plantations. The new trees—conifers—were tall and thin, swaying like high grass in the wind, jostling for the light at the top. There were straight wide lanes for enormous machinery, muddy wheel tracks sinking down two or three feet, and gigantic drainage ditches. To cross them you had to climb down, walk across, then climb up again. As industrial concerns, the new forests were as badly run as most other Soviet industries, whilst the old forest was as decayed and mysterious as the old buildings and forgotten spaces of Soviet cities. It felt abandoned and wild, criss-crossed by forgotten roads leading to abandoned farmhouses, orchards merging with forest, nature taking over.

I soon felt deeply at home in that landscape. I knew that northern Baltic terrain so well, and this was a deeper, vaster, and sadder version of what I had known in Sweden. It was as if I had grown up in Plato's cave, and was now, for the first time, seeing real wilderness. In reality, of course, it was a wilderness of neglect and abandonment, haphazardly re-wilded, not truly wild. I walked for hours, tasting the plants as I walked. In the spring there was wild sorrel—a lost taste since I left Sweden—and later cranberries, bilberries, crowberries, and blackberries.

On the fringes of the forest in August children were playing in clouds of languid late-season mosquitoes. It was very quiet. Occasionally you might hear the roar of a motorised saw, rusty sawing wheels set into old tables. Away from the villages the wilderness crept in, but even there the evidence of war and depopulation was everywhere. I found abandoned farmhouses deep in the forest— mossy thatched roofs caved in, windows partly boarded up, grey animal shades melting into the dusky background. There were wells with rusty buckets, empty tin mugs left on the ground, old orchards now merging with the forest, broken carts, upside-down tin baths half covered with nettles. Beyond, the deep forest was easy to get lost in, dense and green in summer. In the autumn, the human landscape became more evident. Like the ruined teeth in the mouths of older people, the abandoned houses were political signs in that haunted landscape.

Inside the abandoned farmhouses there might be a narrow iron bedstead in the corner of a room, a small table and a stool or chair. The roofs were leaking; old mattresses left behind chewed to pieces. Once I found an old suit and a coat on a bed, grey, poor, and worn out. There was the envelope of a letter, dated 1966. On the floor was an empty can of Russian fly killer. I cautiously walked into the next room, where the rain was dripping steadily through the roof. The kitchen, dark and poor, had a stove, a small table, and a cupboard. It's possible that the former occupants had died, but they might have moved into a flat in the new blocks, or moved away altogether, for whatever reason.

No one ever commented on those abandoned houses. People took it for granted that houses might eventually be abandoned, and that they then naturally decayed, joining the order of nature. In England, where I live now, everything is owned; there is a potential market for every building in the land, and enclosure, beyond the enclaves of national reserves and a few parks and commons, is permanent. That was not the case in the Soviet Union. Within a Western liberal democracy, the signs of war and depopulation would have been gone within a decade; here, as in the old East Berlin, facades scarred by machine guns, they lingered. There was a great poignancy in that. I felt, also, a great sense of freedom walking in those unfenced tracts of land, the freedom of rambling that I had grown up with in Sweden.

The land had not been so accessible during the Soviet occupation. Soon after the war the Soviet authorities ploughed an intermittent deep line in the sandy soil fifty meters from the sea, beyond which people were no longer allowed to go: the entire peninsula, along with most of the Estonian coast, had become classified as a "border protection zone." You needed permission to enter, and identity papers were checked at the barrier. The coastline was dotted with watchtowers, swept by strong searchlights, and the beaches were regularly patrolled.

The authorities tore up a lot of the old juniper and heather, and replaced them with conifer plantations. The inefficiency of the system, in this respect, was a blessing: much of the old forest was left untouched. Even so, many patches of heather and juniper were destroyed. People had watched helplessly as the landscape was transformed before their eyes. I had vivid dreams about this, drenched in that helplessness. I dreamt, also, about soldiers, fear, violence, and hiding, but the dreams about the destruction of the landscape felt more real, I suppose because I had felt that same emotion when I was young, seen the same landscape in Sweden scarred by development.

Protecting the landscape was part of the national conversation in the 1960s and 1970s in Sweden. There was still much common land, treated quite cavalierly by councils everywhere. My father, ever a libertarian, took us children on a secret mission one night, to tear up the awful conifers planted by the council in tidy rows to make some small profit from the previously wild and sandy heather and juniper slope near our weekend house. I was protective of all life as a child, and a little concerned even for those invading conifers as I carefully lifted them from the ground, my father storming ahead. But I was, also, genuinely saddened by the death of that lovely patch of moorland. Once it was gone, there was nothing left to protect, and the council eventually sold the land for housing development, as perhaps it had planned to all along.

The Red Army headquarters were on the grounds of the old Paslepa manor house on the peninsula, which had been demolished after the war. At the time of my fieldwork the flimsy postwar barracks had recently been abandoned, and an Estonian flag had replaced the Soviet one. Under the flagpole was a low white wall where you could still see the faint blue outline of a Soviet map, with a Soviet slogan, in red, underneath: THE BORDERS OF OUR MOTHER-LAND ARE HOLY. A strangely religious slogan, but there it was, Cyrillic letters fading.

There was an archaeology of signs in the landscape, marking the fields and forests, and the small, neat vegetable gardens around the farmhouses. Those gardens were the private plots, well tended and still productive, that each collective farmer was allowed to keep and cultivate. The collective farm fields on the peninsula, by contrast, were too large for the sandy soil, corroded by dusty winds, whilst the giant collective farm machinery, dying icons of Soviet modernity, rusted behind the workshops.

The ploughed line in the sand near the sea was still discernible in places. The watchtowers still stood, stripped and weathered, not yet historical landmarks, but no longer structures of authority. They all had that indeterminate Soviet look, between incompletion and dilapidation: white brick badly put together, concrete poured on the ground to form haphazard paths, woodwork rotting on the platforms, signs in Russian rusting on the floors, long since stripped of wire and anything else of value.

In September, school started. On the first day there were two separate opening ceremonies, one for the younger village children and one for the high school students. The little children marched in to piano music from the Swedish films of Pippi Longstocking. Estonia had allied itself to an international European culture in order to escape the Soviet images of Estonian nationhood: women with corn-blond hair in colourful folk costumes. The music from Pippi Longstocking—instantly recognisable to all Swedes—was yet another way of building Swedishness.

The high school students were different, many of them boarders from other areas. In the evening there was a ceremonial initiation of the new students by the older ones, who were dressed up, or dressed down, in dressing gowns and rags. There was something chilling about the ceremony, which took place in the cold and echoing gym. Some of the pupils were bumped down the stairs, blindfolded, in old shopping trolleys. They were made to sit in buckets of cold water. One boy was subjected to a mock execution, a noose placed around his neck. What it symbolised was unclear, but it was hard not to associate it with the history of Soviet repression. I watched it with Katarina, the new teacher sent out by the Swedish Council, the daughter of a sea captain. She was a beautiful and somewhat ravaged woman in her fifties, with hooded blue eyes.

"Mmm," she said with an indefinable expression. "Well."

She was, generally, an advocate of the common Swedish notion that the troubles of the world could be avoided if only people could be made to see the error of their ways, and become more rational and instrumentalist, more Swedish, in fact, in their political culture. Like me—actually more than me—she cleaned incessantly. But she had unexpected qualities. She tamed a resident mouse by feeding it, and named it Dumble. I knew I was not capable of such a leap into the wild, but I liked it in her.

After the ceremony we went, for the first time, for a drink at the basement bar, Gorbyland. It was small and cosy, selling Western chocolates, ice cream, cigarettes, and packets of coffee as well as Russian and Estonian vodka, sangria, Soviet liqueurs, and beer. Smoking was banned, because of the asthmatic tendencies of Werner, the owner, so there was always a steady stream of smokers going in and out, meeting on the damp concrete steps outside. That night there were about ten men and three boys there, silently watching a Russian videotape of *Teenage Mutant Ninja Turtles*, cheaply and probably illegally dubbed by one bored voice making only the slightest pretence of drama.

To deepen my relationship with the community, I had decided to move out from the "hotel." I had found, through the school, a room with a family. The mother, Inna, was a janitor at the school. Toivo, her husband, was a stonecutter by trade, and was now unemployed, with damaged lungs. They had two children, Ene, a quiet girl of thirteen, and Erki, who was a tough guy of fifteen. That evening, Katarina and I walked past Toivo, who stood, drunk and glassy-eyed, by himself. As we sat down by the bar he came in and stood behind me, and got another drink. I asked if he wanted to sit, and he grabbed my arm quite hard saying no, and whispered, ominously, that he would see me tomorrow. Katarina looked at me with some concern, whilst the rest of the people in the bar studiously ignored us. The Ninja Turtles ran around on the screen, the monotonous Russian voice droning on.

The next day Toivo turned up at midday, drunk and maudlin, strong but unsteady, and said in broken English, "My wife said, my son said, my daughter said, 'No drink,' and now I drink, I drink one, two, three, four drink. Sigrid! I am sorry. I drink. I don't know. Every day I say, 'Tomorrow, no drink.' Every day, drink." I smiled briskly, secretly wary—he was a big man, with a dark beard, and he was not sober. Together we carried my few belongings into the car and drove the short distance across the square to his flat in one of the older blocks opposite the school. Inna, his wife—dark, round, and small—was visibly angry with him, and so was Kulla, their friend and an English teacher at the school. She was an energetic blonde in her forties who, despite her profession, spoke little or no English. She had turned up at the flat a few minutes after I arrived to help to welcome me. I had been given Toivo and Inna's bedroom, and they now slept behind a screen in the living room.

I slowly unpacked, surveying the bed—narrower than any bed I had ever seen, and drowning now in the king-sized duvet and expensive pillows I had bought at NK, the Harrods of Stockholm. One, I remember, was stuffed with lambswool. My friend Johanna had laughed helplessly at my lambswool pillow, and so had I. That pillow, lying there on the narrow bed, seemed to hold the memory of that careless laughter, that easy stepping in and out of expensive shops.

I had been given the ninth grade, the last class of local elementary school, and one class of high school students to teach. I liked teaching, especially the older students, who were interested, and wanted to learn. For the younger ones I used the Soviet school books. They were full of propaganda, which the children tittered about, putting on voices as I had them read passages out loud in class:

> The Soviet Union is a very big country. The people of the Soviet Union want to live and work in peace. They want to live in peace with all the other peoples of the world.
>
> The birthday of the Soviet Union is on the seventh of November. It is a holiday for everybody. The workers do not go to work and the pupils do not go to school. In the morning everybody wants to go to the demonstration. In the afternoon a lot of people have parties. They dance and sing. Some people want to have a rest at home. They usually watch TV or read books. Some people go for long walks with their friends and families. Everybody has a good time. Everybody is happy and cheerful on that day.
> Long live peace!
> Long live Soviet Estonia!
> Long live the Soviet Union!
> Long live Red October Day!

I pointed at the next girl to read more:

Exercise 1: Translate
1. Skilled workers are needed everywhere.
2. Educated people are needed to develop our socialist culture.
3. Every year all-republican contests are held in mathematics.
4. Prizes are given to the winners of contests.
5. Mathematics is taught at school.
6. Estonian is spoken in the Estonian SSR.

7. Russian is spoken all over the Soviet Union.
8. In the Soviet Union the young people are given every opportunity for many-sided development.

They giggled even more at that, glancing at each other and at me. It was hard to believe that this was only two years after it ended.

I was now immersing myself in Estonian. I had endured many hours of Estonian language training with a young Estonian teacher at the School of Slavonic and East European Studies in London. I was her only pupil, but the school prided itself on the many languages it offered. She never, I think, really understood my project—after several lessons it emerged that she thought that my prospective "field work" meant that I was going to assist the collective farmers in their farm work, probably for an agricultural study. She smiled at me with slightly empty blue eyes, and proceeded to drill the language into me, until I nearly cried with frustration. Estonian, along with Finnish and Hungarian, is notoriously difficult to learn. It's not a tonal language, and not part of the Indo-European family. Its grammar is so complex that one feels it could only have been invented in the north, tribal elders and their assistants honing the complexity of the language through the dark nights of winter.

We had no books, and my teacher would bring me sheets of vocabulary. The first lesson I looked at the photocopy in front of me and started laughing slightly hysterically because I recognised not a *single* word on the sheet. I had studied many European languages—English, of course, but also French, German, and Italian—but I had never before learnt a language that was not Indo-European. Learning Estonian made me feel that I had only ever really studied dialects of the same language before, Latin and Germanic roots casually intertwined. This was like learning random strings of code by heart, with whimsical comic interludes of phonetic loan words like *peekon* for "bacon." The older Swedish or German loanwords often had the initial *s* or *st* dropped off. Thus *strand* ("beach"), becomes *rand*; *stund* ("a while," or "an hour"), *tund*; *storm*, *torm*; and so on, creating an oddly childlike atmosphere within the complexity.

All the flats in the village were strikingly alike, differing only in degrees of modernity. Toivo and Inna's block had been built in the 1960s, halfway between the ones built in the 1950s— wood stoves and wooden staircases—and the later ones, which were of a better material standard. It had running water, but the lavatory was a waterless, sinister hole. The interiors, however, were the same in all the flats—a living room with a sofa and some chairs, a wall unit with a television, books, dried flowers, and glass animals. In the bathrooms and kitchens, empty Western bottles and packages, presents from visitors, were displayed as decorations. In Toivo and Inna's flat, empty bottles of Charm fabric conditioner, "Simply Satin," and Russian eau de cologne, as well as Swedish and Finnish shampoo, and an empty Colgate tube, were arranged on the bathroom shelf. During my survey of the community, I came across only one unusual decoration: a collection of beer cans, arranged in a pyramid. I thought it was unique, until, a few days later, I saw a similar collection, identically arranged. The idea of expressing individualism through materialism, and the idea of competing via material goods—two fundamental ideas of Western societies—were pretty absent on the collective farm. When the villagers displayed empty Western shampoo bottles, they did so in the knowledge that Western bottles had become accepted forms of decoration, not in order to compete with their neighbours. Those bottles were signs that the whole village had a connection with the West, a way of expressing the new normal.

Toivo and Inna's books were quality stuff, and this was not unusual either. There, in Soviet hardback editions, was Balzac's *Père Goirot*, John Galsworthy's *The Forsyte Saga*, Thomas Hardy's *The*

Mayor of Casterbridge, Erich Remarque's *Arc de Triomphe,* and Jack London's *Martin Eden*; Bernard Shaw, Emile Zola, John Gardner, Gerald Durrell, Guy de Maupassant, and Franz Kafka. They also had Vladimir Nabokov's *Lolita* and Alexander von Bülow's *Passion*; Ian Fleming, the Norwegian author Trygve Gulbranssen, and Alberto Moravia (who was published in the Soviet Union); a Pat Conroy thriller; a Swedish-Estonian dictionary; a book on astrology and a dream interpretation book. Toivo and Inna didn't read books, or newspapers, or anything other than, occasionally, the dictionary, to help me in my halting Estonian conversations. I don't think I ever really understood the point of that personal library, but I think it had to do with Soviet notions of high culture, of the ceaseless Soviet struggle to combat "rural idiocy," and, also, with censorship and the normativity of cultural life. *Lolita* was banned in the Soviet Union until 1989, so that must have been new. Ian Fleming, I assume, was new. The older books, the Soviet classics, came with the territory—cheap, ubiquitous, and unread. The best that could be said for them was that if one day a bookish child would be born into one of the village families, those hardback editions of the classics would be ready and waiting.

It was a surprise to me to find that the villagers were so lacking in materialism and materialist aspirations. They really did live in a more immediate and experiential world. The scene, as it were, was already set. The props were simple and accepted as such, the quality of the play not judged by the simplicity of the stage set. Now, however, that expensive Western goods were arriving in dribs and drabs, the material life of the collective farm was beginning to look and feel poor and tawdry in comparison. The empty bottles on the bathroom shelves in the village, and on shelves across western Estonia, were originally modest gifts from Swedish visitors. They couldn't have predicted that the utilitarian soap and shampoo they brought would have the effect of making the Soviet-quality shampoo seem forever not good enough. They couldn't have foreseen that their presents of Swedish coffee would make Estonian coffee taste thin and bitter, or that their very presence on the collective farm would make the villagers feel poor and provincial in comparison.

The logic of the gift, in anthropological terms, is that the giver is enriched, whilst the recipient is placed in a position of obligation, of social debt. The Swedes, coming from a deeply egalitarian culture, followed this logic by often appearing dimly ashamed of their gifts and of seeming too rich, and yet they felt they should bring something. It was complicated. Sometimes people avoided the issue by giving me the gifts instead of the villagers. Other times I was given things because the visitors thought I was a villager. I got a hat, chewing gum, coffee, and vitamins. I declined a computer. I remember opening a bottle of vitamin C someone hastily thrust into my hand. The dusty sour smell of it made my mouth water, and I couldn't quite bring myself to explain the mistake and return it, though I think—I hope—I did pass it on.

One day in September a Swedish family arrived in a red Volvo loaded with IBM computers. They had persuaded IBM Sweden to donate eight older models to the community. Four were supposed to go to the school and four to the municipal authorities. I went with them to the mayor's office to see one of them set up, a gleaming white computer on the land surveyor's old desk, next to an untidy heap of ancient-looking documents. Actually the documents, lists of farms being reclaimed by former refugees, were more recent than the computers, which in Sweden were already deemed to be obsolete.

The family came from one of the villages, and had applied to get their old house back. I turned the conversation to the house claims and the list of farms. The woman, who was the applicant, knew most of the names on the list. Recently they'd had a meeting in Sweden, with more than four hundred people there. The Estonian Swedish organisation Svenska Odlingens Vänner (Friends of Swedish Culture), which was enjoying a post-Soviet revival, had informed the audience when to apply and how. She took a long time answering my question about whether they will get the house back, and seemed uncertain about who lived there now: a Russian man, she said, and a woman, "some kind of half Russian."

The land surveyor tinkered helplessly with the computer, and finally said he would get somebody from the already computerised land office in Haapsalu to come and help . I wondered what would happen to the computers. The Swedes were concerned that they shouldn't get into the wrong hands, and then offered one of them to me, which, though obviously the wrong hands, was not surprising. Much later, the computers were indeed lost, though how I don't know.

Earlier a group of Swedish Finns from Kronoby, the Finnish twin town, had come for a visit. One of them gave me a woolly hat as a present. In the evening they came for an event at the culture house with some locals, including Alar, the other English teacher, who, unlike Kulla, could actually speak English. Virve, the Swedish teacher from Finland, looked on in silence. She was Finnish, but spoke Swedish fluently, a serious and cultured person, probably then in her late fifties. She didn't think much of my project, I think, but eventually warmed to me enough to voice her complaints about the mismanagement of the Swedish revival. Inna, the school secretary, was behind the bar, selling vodka, beer, and liqueurs, cake and black smoked flatfish. Werner from Gorbyland, playing a synthesiser, started the singing and dancing. A small elderly Finnish man came up to me and asked me to dance, alarmingly flirtatious. "Do you go on holiday ever?" he asked. "To the Canaries?" He held me tight, and I was overwhelmed with waves of slightly hysterical laughter. The Finnish women danced together, the Estonians danced in tight and old-fashioned couples. No one mixed much. I drank a glass of Vana Tallinn, Estonian sweet and smoky brandy, and felt cold and nauseated later. The Finns left, expressing concern for me, who would have to stay behind in the village after they had gone. I thought of the many times in my life when I had been the one to leave, visiting aid projects, feeling concern for those who stayed behind. Now it was me trudging back to my cold room, going to sleep and waking up in the same reality. And it wasn't too bad.

Perhaps not surprisingly, given the impoverishment that the new system had brought, the majority of the people on the collective farm thought the old system was better than the new one. Ironically, in the beginning of my fieldwork, the caution bred by Soviet repression meant that this preference was communicated to me in code rather than in open conversation. Being openly discontented would have demonstrated opposition to the authorities, still thought to be more powerful than perhaps they actually were. I soon understood that people generally assumed that my fieldwork involved an element of spying on behalf of the village authorities, not least since I was obviously not particularly interested in what they thought I should be interested in—the ethnography of pre-war Estonian Swedish life—and overly interested in Soviet and post-Soviet matters that were still of political relevance. Even though dissidence and political repression were a thing of the past, Soviet habits of thought were taking some time to wash out of the system.

Thus in the beginning of my fieldwork, people talked cautiously about the lack of "work" and "bread" (always *leib*, or "dark bread," as opposed to *sai*, "white bread")—evocative terms, embedded in the old slogan "Work and bread for the people!" Unemployment was high. Women moved into the category of "housewife," but men without work were invariably *töötu*, "unemployed," said with a shrug, gazing at the floor, or defiantly, with a stare: *This is what your great system has brought us.* Gradually, stories of corruption and opportunism emerged, stories that may never be properly investigated. There were no proper channels for complaints or whistle-blowing yet, and protests would probably lead nowhere.

I was later told that one of my informants had been accused of having collaborated with the KGB. I remembered being surprised at seeing quite so much of this particular person in the official photographs from the *kolkhoz* time. I remembered him one summer day in his little Škoda, stopping the car in a cloud of dust, beckoning me over to give me some strawberries. His wife was drinking beer from a bottle next to him, there was a gaggle of kids in the back; the day was hot, dusty, almost hallucinatory. It was easy, in the repressed atmosphere of the collective farm, where so much still was not said, to imagine scenes of collaboration. It may have been true, I don't know.

By mid-September I was fully settled in with Toivo and Inna. Their little Scottish terrier had taken to me in a big way—I was the first person in his life to take him for walks, and he appreciated that enormously. I was covered in fleabites as a result. On 22 September my diary records that there was some tepid water in the morning. This was rare: the water had been cold since I arrived. I took a brief and trickling shower, and Inna washed clothes in the tub.

Toivo continued to drink, and was sentimental and maudlin when drunk. "I have a brother, and now I have a sister, Sigrid, you," he said. "I look at you, a beautiful woman, and I understand you." Inna looked worried, and, I have to say, so was I. On this occasion, and on many others to come, I distracted them by making them laugh. That wasn't hard—there was so much I didn't know, and so much I didn't understand, and all of that was potentially funny. There is no dignity in fieldwork, only constant engagement.

One evening Toivo rang his friend Ets, a builder and sailor, and father of one of my pupils. Toivo was, intermittently, working for him. Ets was not local; he had moved to the peninsula from Kohtla-Järve, because, he said, of the tension there between the Estonians and the Russians. That evening he came to be introduced to me, bringing a bottle of strawberry liqueur. I sipped it cautiously, and we talked.

"How old are you, may I ask?" he asked politely. I said thirty-one. "And not married?" His intense blue eyes were studying me, a small man with some sort of authority. I was suddenly so happy that my breath was catching, the delirious happiness of feeling that the fieldwork was going to be possible after all. It was possible to break through the silence, and have comprehensible conversations. And, of course, the tipsy sweet happiness of strawberry liqueur.

FIVE

The Mercy of God

One day I met an old woman who was carrying a small, pale child on the back of an old bicycle. She knew who I was—I think by then everyone did, though most people still ignored me. She, instead, addressed me in broken Swedish: "The mercy of God is great." She looked at me expectantly and patiently with intelligent blue eyes.

"Are you Swedish?" I asked in Estonian, but she shook her head. She was Estonian and a Seventh-day Adventist. That day, standing outside the shop, she talked to me in a mixture of four languages about her life. The child, purple shadows under her eyes, sat waiting quietly.

Later Ruth came to visit me again, and I got to know her better. She was seventy-six, and had been married twice. She had had six children, and was originally from Haapsalu. She told me in broken German about the hard and punitive work on the collective farm after the war. Nobody was paid then, and women had to carry the heavy milk containers. One Christmas Eve she and some other women known to be religious were forced to clean out the pigsties. The authorities burnt all the Bibles they could find outside the church that year, she said. I was still living in the "hotel" then, and there was an eerie moment when Timo came in. She looked at me with obvious fear, and started to shuffle the papers she had brought with her. After that she whispered. Timo, wholly indifferent to Soviet matters, couldn't have cared less, but I could see that he might have randomly resembled a Soviet apparatchik from that time, so smooth and blond, something inscrutable about him.

A few days later I visited Ruth at her cottage. She waited for me outside. We stood in her tiny vegetable garden, the grey geese collecting in the field across the meadow, hundreds of them gathering under the high sky before flying south. As we stood there, she talked, again, about her past, a life of oppression and poverty. Her husband was the deputy chairman of the collective farm, and a violent and abusive alcoholic. Despite his privileged position, she worked in the dairy, backbreaking labour because of the heavy canisters, in the reek of souring milk.

One day in 1952 she fainted at work, and woke up to hallucinations, including a vision of Stalin, dead, lying in his grave. She saw the school in the village in flames, a vision that would also soon be fulfilled—the old school was, indeed, later consumed by fire. She saw, too, all the many records of surveillance, interviews with informers and interrogations incriminating local people, sucked up in a whirlwind above the manor house, then the communist headquarters—a vision that did not come true. Where was she, then, I wondered, on that fine line between religion, dissidence, and mental illness? She must, at least, have felt free, the freedom that madness brings in totalitarianism, because when her co-workers gathered around her, she told them what she saw. She was also, suddenly, paralysed.

She was hospitalised in a clinic in town. One morning her husband came in drunk. He shouted at her, and at everyone else within hearing distance, that she was "anti-communist," and staggered up to her and hit her. "*Contra kommunismus—Ich könnte das nicht verstehen—das vare ju guilliotin* [Against communism—I couldn't understand it—that was the guillotine]," she whispered in her broken German, and drew her hand across her throat. But he himself was on another borderline, between the violent world of the paranoid alcoholic and the relative security and power of his position. The authorities probably wanted to get rid of him—in his own way I imagine he was as much of a liability as Ruth. Whatever discussions may have taken place in the background, after the episode at the clinic, he was sent to a centre for alcoholics in Tallinn.

Eventually they both came home. The paralysis subsided, and Ruth was working again, subdued and resigned. The treatment hadn't cured her husband's drinking, and life was as hard as before. One day, in the vegetable garden, he lost his temper, and raised his arm to hit her, when out of nowhere a KGB man stepped in, and took him away. She was, of course, reluctant to see a KGB man as an angelic messenger, but nevertheless she felt a sense of divine intervention about the way he appeared at that particular moment. They were under surveillance, presumably, and it was probably as good a time as any to arrest him. Later she was arrested, too, and sent to a "reeducation" camp in southern Estonia. She escaped from there, and, helped by her daughter, came back to the peninsula, at first clandestinely. Within months she was arrested again, interrogated, beaten, and sent back to the camp. After Stalin's death in 1953 she was rehabilitated. She came back to the house, and continued to work in the dairy.

Her husband, who by then had come back, died from alcoholism not long afterwards. She eventually married again, but this time it was a calling—God asked her to marry a man who was disabled, and she did. She was, when I knew her, deeply, perhaps even madly, religious. She was also unusually intelligent, sensitive, and creative. The pressure of Stalinism, and in fact the virtual embodiment of Stalinism in the coarse and violent form of her husband, and the grim suffering she endured, flipped her, I think, over the edge, and she never quite recovered.

We had slowly approached her house from the meadow where she had directed me to put the car. She walked backwards, looking at me intently, into the garden, which was fenced with uneven poles of wood to keep the elk and the wild boar out. "*Die sind böse tieren,*" she said about the boars, "evil animals." We stood on the uneven steps of the cottage for at least half an hour, by two old tin baths collecting rainwater. Finally she lifted the rusty chain from its hook and we went in.

It was like entering a cave. I carefully stepped into the hall, and she closed the door, lined on the inside with dirty rags. The walls, too, were lined with bundles of wood and torn rags. From this surreal and narrow passage we entered the kitchen, through a low doorway. The kitchen was a bare room, with an old wood-fired range and a bench. The floor was covered with bits of wood and scraps of fabric. There was an electrical radiator with slices of bread drying on it, and a tin bucket with more bread on the floor. There was no other food, though she did grow apples, potatoes, cabbage, and beetroot in her garden. She slowly escorted me through the kitchen, to her bedroom beyond.

Here, she had an iron bed, a table, and a chair. There were many religious books on the table, all of them open, some carefully mended, and some annotated in her handwriting. There were juniper branches everywhere. This stopped the mice and rats from eating the books, she said, and showed me how they had eaten away some of the paper. Those dismal bite marks explained the odd shapes of the pages of the book she had given me earlier—she must have trimmed the pages nibbled by vermin. I sat on the chair and she sat on the bed, talking about God. I had given her a packet of Swedish biscuits, which she held in her hand during the entire visit, incongruous clear yellow in this environment where everything merged into a dark blue brown. The windows were almost boarded up, torn pieces of lace and rags stuck on the boards. In the end she called me "Liebe Sigrid," and blessed me.

Now, so many years later, I feel the limitation of words: "apples," "beetroot," and "cabbage," the produce of her garden, are such pleasant words, organic and wholesome. How do you convey the poverty? Not only hers, but the poverty of most of the old people I met: old European peasant poverty. The smell of stale sweat, earth, and apples. How can I describe her obvious trauma, the marks that the Stalinist repression had left on her? Her tears, and the tears of other old people, when they talked about the arrests, the forced collectivisation and the deportations. Veevi usually got angry with me as she remembered, and I responded as best I could. "'Really?' you say—yes, really, that is how we lived!" she would say, glaring at me. Ruth and the other old people on the collective farm were never angry. Their subterranean memories of those desperate times of long ago were painful, and they often cried, but they were too patient, and too submissive, for anger.

Ruth was also, of course, an eccentric within the community on the peninsula. In Estonian Seventh-day Adventist circles, however, she was quite well known, and had been mentioned in a book, which she modestly showed me. She had also written a tract herself, *Leib Taevast* ("[Dark] Bread from Heaven"), published in 1988. She had, also, created a little museum on the first floor of her house, dedicated to the Swedish missionary Ölvingsson, who had lived there. The first floor had been left almost as it was when he escaped from Estonia with his wife during the war, their few belongings arranged and regularly dusted. She only showed me that the following summer—it was an act of trust, and it took her a long time to trust me.

About a week after I first met her, I visited Ruth again. I remember sitting on her bed, a pile of small worm-eaten apples by my feet, an old-fashioned alarm clock ticking on the table. Part of the wall was covered by wallpaper, and there was a picture of a snowy mountain landscape from an English almanac from 1977. Old books, again, were open everywhere, almost like decorations. Torn old clothes were hanging in a corner. At a certain point she started to sing from the kitchen, in a high beautiful voice, an Estonian hymn. She was cooking for me, peeling potatoes, whilst singing the unexpectedly beautiful song. When it was all done—boiled potatoes, burnt black cabbage, and sour cream on a tin plate, cabbage soup with potatoes and carrots in a tin bowl, and stewed apples—she covered my legs with a white cloth and watched me eat, her blue eyes shining.

She told me then about reading Billy Graham years ago, at Christmas, by candlelight. The electricity had been cut off, and no one knew she was there. I felt the poignant distinction between her poverty and her suffering, and the commercial and sanitised blandness of the American evangelists. I took notes as she spoke. "*Nicht schreiben Eesti keeles* [Don't write in Estonian]," she said in a mix of German and Estonian, worried that I would be indiscreet. Estonian was a lasso that would catch her, and a noose, she told me. They always had to write by hand, she said, because the KGB was always looking for typewriters. She looked at me, head to one side, concentrating, and said, in English: "But God gave me wings and made my enemies blind." There was a rustling noise in a corner, a rat or a mouse. God gave her wings. Her mission in life had given her such a profound sense of meaning and purpose. It was her sanity and her insanity.

I left her eventually, and walked into the forest. I glimpsed a fox, and soon I was lost, deep in that familiar Baltic forest, my home. I wandered around for several hours, until I found a road. Eventually someone in a car stopped to give me a lift home. We drove in silence, and I got off on the square nodding my thanks.

Soon afterwards Ruth gave me a handwritten notebook, her "Life Story," and then another one, to help my study. She entitled it "The History of Nuckö," the Swedish name for Noarootsi, the peninsula. These were extraordinary documents, laboriously translated from Estonian into English, which she didn't speak well. The translation, and her slightly feverish state of mind, made them unintentionally beautiful, even poetic. "Life Story" was mainly a religious tract, mixed with local history. She never wrote down what she told me about her own life, unfortunately. "The History of Nuckö" was a description of the peninsula as it had been before the Soviet invasion. Within the madness, and the crazy translation, was reality; and the madness, and the translation, was also a reflection of the reality and the history that she endured. Her eccentricity—I don't think it was more than that, in the beginning—was precipitated through historical circumstances into mental illness, her difference a part of the twentieth-century story of this peninsula, this collective farm, and the Soviet regime. Ruth is dead now—she died a few years after I left Estonia.

Extracts from Ruth Kanarbik's "Life Story," Pürksi, October 18, 1993

I begin to write over Pasklep. Devilish age, sad age. Schoolchildren also spies, sky was as night, earth as giddiness, deceit, fraud—life as leprosy. Communist live royally. Work women (people) must live as deaf and dumb. Wherever seen wrong, evil, crime underfed always naked (footwear old, rubbers broken) cold habit, children only home.

Kommunist was visitor, holiday maker. Kommunism was criminal offender, delinquent, felon, stupid reign. Very, very great baseness, cruelty, arrogance! Yes it is stupidity! Kommunism (is sinister) is learned to murder (murderer).

Alcohol is youth's glutton and snake. God give happiness and lucky and blessing, but alcohol is a great misfortune, mishap . . . alcohol is a bullet, a gunpowder to the people, the youth.

University pitch-dark, to mock wise, sage, intelligent people.

I wish to witness, to speak what God did to Nuckö (Noarootsi). Historie speak a sea was over Nuckö, then a little island, a small islet. Then sea go silently away, earth came, to come in sight.

God present to Nuckö one richness. This is: sea mud (mire, slime) medicine to cure. Near Nuckö is town Haapsalu, this is a little kuurort—summer-resort. Histoire speak: Nuckö beautiful Ramsholm was full visitor—to spend the summer. Nuckö near Wormsi have in sea many, many, many ton sea mud. (+ raadium)

This seamud to bring to sanatorim and there is people coming to cure (to treat). This liquid, fluid seamud is cure with water in bath, and in baths. Salty sea mud baths. Must money to give and illness go better.

Nuckö is rich apple-trees and apples. Also wicker-work, wicker chair. And many, many plum-trees. Sortiment: "Noarootsi red plum." This name is good sortiment over Estonia.

In Nuckö is God very beautiful woods to present. Many, many linden trees (lime trees) For example: medicine-trees: pine trees, great pine woods. Pine-cones! Chestnut trees!

Very good potatoes earth. Nuckö in Estonian age to bring—to carry, to transport potatoes to Sweden, and red plums and rye (cornflower blew). Every farmer transport this material to Sweden.

Many farmer was fisher. Fishmarket was in Haapsalu town. Fishing season was fishy.

Motorboat little (ship) bring people in Österby harbour every day three time in town Haapsalu. There in Österby is stone warf, pier. A long iron-stone bridge.

In Nuckö is a beautiful flora. Interesting! Vegetation, is very medicine plant.

Plentiful berry earth, many storms. Stormy days. Red-berry in wood (no strawberry). Bilberry, blueberry. Very medicine. Whortleberry. Very good jem (dzemm) with apples. Very delicate. This all is God Present. Say God price! Honour!

Also give good Sky Father in Nuckö the people and children red winter berry in swampy, in marshy, boggi. This winterberry is cranberry . . . here is red baburitsky berry. This berry wish cold water over to power and sinking over. Oo that is very tasteful, delicious, palatable! Oo how pleasant soür, acid. That is medical berry.

In Nuckö is very good flower-base (platform) the bee-keeping. Many kilograms honey and bee life is good, very little illness. I was (have) also years bee-keeping.

In Nuckö is also wolf, they came, when communism came to Estonia. All unfit, unfitness, immoral, improper came in Nuckö with atheism and red-armee military. And military state of war. That was terrible! Our home was near sea, near Wormsi bay. There was three kilometer frontier guard. Border-land-territory. No one step can people no go.

Mysterious reign, secret, to dissimulate, clandestine.

So to mask GPU. He as jackal to carry women (men) despair, despondency, desperate.

There are hints here of a thriving rural pre-war economy. The war, and the Soviet system, ended it all. The ferry, which left for Haapsalu three times a day from the harbour, was long since gone. The trade in wickerwork and apples, potatoes, plums, honey, and rye was all gone. Private fishing was banned after the Soviet take-over, and the fish market in Haapsalu closed down. The spa and the tourists were gone.

The vibrant rural civil society of the 1930s was also gone: the agricultural mutual benefit societies and cooperatives, choirs and sport clubs, sobriety meetings and libraries, Swedish minority schools and journals, and, of course, independent farming. By 1993 the sea was too dirty to fish, and the huge, useless collective farm fields, brushed by dusty winds, were lying fallow, waiting to be claimed by former owners, the former refugees. Old people fitfully remembered that lost world, that particular social economy. Young people didn't know much, if anything, about it.

Six

History

Before my fieldwork I had visited the Estonian Swedish group Svenska Odlingens Vänner in Stockholm, located in a basement flat in a respectable residential area. It was run by two émigrés, a woman from Noarootsi and a man from Ormsö, or Vormsi in Estonian. The society had eked out an émigré cultural existence since the war, but now, with the revival of the Estonian Swedish culture, they were busy, advising on property claims, organising events, and talking to journalists. But the aesthetic of that basement—salmon-coloured walls, glass cabinet with mannequins in folk costumes bleached blond hair and curled eyelashes thick with mascara—was of the 1970s, when no one wanted to know about the Estonian Swedes.

The man, I remember, told me a story about seeing a Swedish ethnographic film about Ormsö in Sweden, shortly after his arrival. He noticed, and the audience, he assumed, did too, that the legs of one of the women in the film were dirty, and he felt such shame about the dirt and the poverty, and the strange folk costumes. I felt for him. But soon after the war nobody was watching those old films anymore anyway. The culture of the Estonian Swedes was over. The Nazi taint had corroded the curiosity about the Estonian Swedish minority, and the fact that Swedes had once lived in Estonia was gradually forgotten.

After my year in Estonia I came back to read their journals and books, and to learn more about the lost pre-war culture of the Estonian Swedes. Stockholm, so brash and commercial after Estonia, confused me then. The pink basement was a refuge, and I delved into the history.

The first Swedish revival in Estonia, I learnt, started with a mission. Between 1873 and 1887, five evangelical missionaries were sent to the Estonian Swedish settlements. One of them, a man called Österblom, wrote a book about his stay on Ormsö, an island near Noarootsi.

The island of Ormsö was owned by the Swedish Baron von Stackelberg. There were at that time more than two thousand people on the island, nearly all Swedish-speaking. They were hard-drinking, poor people—landless peasants working for the oppressive Stackelberg in return for food. A few decades before the mission a Swedish ship ran ashore on the wintry island, and the baron invited the captain to stay. The captain saw people driven off the road into a snowdrift, and kneeling down in the snow to make way for the baron, who shouted and lashed out at them with his whip. Even the serfs in Russia, the captain wrote, were less enslaved: "At least you would see them happy, and hear them sing; the coastal Estonians, or Swedes, as they are still called, did not know any songs and did not seem to know what happiness was."

The islanders were ravaged by alcohol and poverty. Shipwrecks were plundered, and theft was common. "During the night the wool was stolen which had been cut during the day," Österblom wrote, "and the seed which should have been sown, and when nothing came of it, it was said that the worms had eaten it. It was vain to employ anyone as a guard, because he would steal more than anyone." He continued: "One speaks about the curse of drinking, but here was a living illustration of it. The people went around dressed in rags.

Dirt, vermin, grief and illness were consuming them." The farm-houses were dirty, and often without chimneys, and the thatched roofs were leaking. "In these smoky and dirty cottages lived up to four families, where each family had a corner of the room, and one bed. One of the men was the farmer, and the others were servants. These servants had no wages, simply food, and some clothes."

Religious freedom was limited. Laymen were not allowed to gather for spiritual purposes except in household prayers, and then they were restricted to reading from the Bible or from Luther's postils. Österblom practised as a teacher, concealing his mission-ary purpose. He began by reading Luther to a small gathering of people, which lulled them to sleep:

> These people were unusually good at sleeping. If they had the opportunity to lie down on a bench, they were soon fast asleep. That they fell asleep during my reading was perhaps natural, since they didn't understand what I read ... When I understood that, I let the book lie open in front of me, and read between the lines instead. I used the same words that they used in their everyday speech, and the same dialect. Then they woke up and became very attentive.

The beginning, however, was slow:

> I talked to everybody I met about the saving of their souls. People therefore became afraid of me, so it wasn't easy to get hold of anyone. If I met someone in the forest, he would steal away amongst the bushes, like a fish diving deeper in the water. Sometimes I would see people climb over stone walls, and walk across the fields to escape me.

Finally one woman was saved, and filled, she said, with ecstasy and peace and joy. Others followed. Now people were torn between

Österblom and the Lutheran priest on the island, or, as some saw it, between anti-Christ and the church: "What was distinctly to my disadvantage was that the seer had predicted that during the year I arrived, anti-Christ would come to Wormsö."

After the first wave of revivals, Österblom called the women to a meeting, where he told them the story of David and Goliath. He told them that Goliath existed on Ormsö, too, and asked them to put up their hand if they wanted to help to defeat him. They were all so eager to help that they put up not one hand but two: "After I thus caught them in the trap, I told them that the *Goliath* I was referring to was *dirt* and *uncleanliness*." He talked to them about the dirt in their homes until they wept, and promised to clean. The next day he set off on a tour of inspection, and saw cottage floors covered in water. The women were digging mud and dirt from the floors to reveal long-forgotten planks. He also encouraged people to build chimneys. Most people had damaged eyes from living in a constant cloud of smoke. After one man saved his eyes by building a chimney, following Österblom's advice, many others soon did the same: "When the smoke and the dirt were done away with," he wrote, "people became very grateful to us."

Österblom was by now revered. He was even called in by the baron to talk to striking villagers, whom he persuaded to go back to work. The mission had transformed the islanders, he wrote, into "honest and sober workers," sought after on the mainland as factory workers, servants, and wet nurses. Gone was their reputation for thievery, laziness, and drunkenness. Before, he wrote, "They often appeared in small groups, dressed in rags, and always begging. You gave them money or whatever they wanted at once, to get them out of your doorway as soon as possible, so as not to catch vermin from them."

This is how quickly cultures can change. Like most Swedes, I had assumed as a child that the Swedish national character was intrinsically solid, hard-working, and egalitarian. Ormsö, in fact, was a kind of microcosm of Sweden at the time: deeply hierarchical, poor, and alcoholic. Individuals in Sweden profoundly transformed that society over the course of a few decades, from the 1890s to the 1930s, just as Österblom transformed Ormsö. Progressive people were active everywhere; the whole of Europe was changing and improving. Cultures are so malleable, so changeable, and also so fragile. What can be created can also be destroyed. If history is falsified, people eventually forget.

As for the mission, it remained controversial. Members of the board of the Swedish Evangelical National Society came to visit, following a number of accusations from the Estonian Evangelical Lutheran Church. A "strong wind of mercy," they wrote in their report, had transformed the island: "As a consequence there is now not a single bar left on this island inhabited by about 2,000 people, and nobody dares to drink and steal publicly, whereas before Ö's arrival there were a large number of bars, and stealing, drinking, and fighting were openly practiced." The mission, they wrote, deserved support:

> . . . particularly since we have here descendants of Swedes, who, even though they have been separated from the motherland in a foreign country for hundreds of years, still speak the Swedish tongue, albeit an ancient form of it, so that the question of language is no hindrance to their education. They have at the occasion of the visitation asked to convey their kindest regards and warmest thanks to the Board and the Friends of the Mission for what has been done for them, and, furthermore, have asked to be included in our prayers.

Opposition, however, continued from the Estonian Evangelical Lutheran Church. In February 1887 the mission, which had then been running for fourteen years, was finally closed down. Österblom was summarily deported from the Russian Empire, following an interview with the governor of Tallinn, Count Scachowskoi. The final accusation was sacrilege: it was alleged that he had claimed to be Jesus Christ.

The poverty, and the impoverished culture, of the Russian Empire was not so different from today's repressive societies. All the ingredients were there: blasphemy laws and censorship, excessive bureaucracy, a secret police and terrorist threats, corruption and oppression of minorities. The nationalist "Russification" measures of the 1880s made life particularly difficult for the ethnic minorities of the Russian Empire. Their languages were banned in schools, and censorship was tightened, to impose the Russian language and culture on the margins of the Empire.

Towards the end of the nineteenth century there were two teachers on Noarootsi, Johan Nymann and Hans Pöhl, who belonged to the Swedish minority. Their secret goal was the "unification" of the Swedes in Russia, but all they could realistically hope for was to establish a small Swedish lending library in Noarootsi. After a lengthy application process permission was granted, on condition that a list of the proposed books was delivered to the local school inspector, who doubled as a censor. There was another long delay whilst the list was inspected. The books, gifts from individuals and societies in Sweden, were already there, hidden in the villages. Everything takes so long in repressive societies. Applications are reviewed with excessive caution when the repercussions of making the wrong decision are harsh. The censor goes through documents and books with his black pen, redacting subversive thought. Books are hidden, secrets are kept, ambitions are thwarted; cultural poverty becomes entwined with material poverty.

Whilst they waited, Nymann and Pöhl investigated what other forms of association might be possible. A temperance society seemed one way to call legitimate meetings, and permission was eventually granted for that. Many issues other than drinking were discussed at those meetings, and potentially subversive contact was made with temperance societies in Sweden. Well-wishers there sent more books, journals, and financial assistance, in solidarity with their compatriots across the Baltic Sea. Finally, of course, there was a crack down: in 1904 Nymann was called in and questioned at the police headquarters in Haapsalu, accused of hiding and lending revolutionary books. By 1905 the controversy of the library reached St. Petersburg, and the decision was taken higher up to ban all Swedish books in Estonia. That year, however, was also the beginning of the end of this phase of Russian imperial oppression. The workers' strikes and, eventually, the revolution of 1905 led to the establishment of Russia's first parliament, the Duma, and a new constitution. The temporary liberalisation was halted by the outbreak of the First World War, but the ideas and, it has to be said, conditions of revolution remained.

The minorities in Estonia were discussing their relationship to the state and majority cultures even before independence in 1918, like minorities in all the countries in the region. Soon the debate about minority rights, about the national aspirations of minorities, about Zionism, about separate schools, about quotas to universities, and so on was taking place in newspapers across eastern and central Europe. The question of what place ethnic minorities occupied in the nation-state was one of the most important central European political questions of the time. The discussions among the Swedes in Estonia were a very small part of a much wider debate.

Some thirty years after Österblom's deportation, before the First World War, an unemployed agronomist called Gunnar Schantz left Sweden for Estonia. He, too, wrote a book about his experiences. He worked initially at a Baltic German estate. The landowners were Baltic German, as were the priests, doctors, and veterinarians. The tenant farmers, stewards, administrators, and superintendents were generally Germanised Estonians who had taken German names. Lowest in the hierarchy were the so-called *Undeutsche*, the Estonian peasants, former serfs. "And the peasant?" he wrote. "I see him walking with slow, well measured steps up the paved walkway to the office, holding his cap with both hands pressed against the chest. His exaggerated submissiveness was completely alien to me as a Swede and filled my heart with bitterness and compassion."

Schantz returned to Sweden after the war, with none of the capital he had hoped to save to buy his own farm, and faced, moreover, with recession and unemployment. After some time he turned to the church and, in 1923, took ordination as a Lutheran pastor. He trained as a missionary, and was soon on his way back to Estonia, this time to the island of Runö (Ruhnu in Estonian). This most remote of the Estonian islands was inhabited entirely by Swedes, who, even before independence, farmed their own land, fished, and traded seal fur and fat. Unusually, they had no landowner, and it was therefore a far more egalitarian society than most of the islands and the mainland. Schantz had had some experience of Estonian Swedes, particularly from Ormsö, who often took temporary work on the mainland estates during the summer. "They were well liked and always welcome," he wrote, seemingly unaware of that island's late nineteenth-century cultural transformation under the guidance of the missionary Österblom

Schantz arrived on Runö in 1923, three years after Estonian independence. The islanders spotted the boat, and went down to the beach. He described the scene: "Children playing, wearing colourful traditional clothes, men and women of all ages, barking dogs, rows of flat wagons each with a pair of small and ragged horses." He brought the islanders hymnbooks and grindstones, tobacco plants and boxes of books, toys, Christmas tree lights, and other gifts. With him were also two researchers from Nordiska Museet, the large ethnographic museum in Stockholm.

The enlightened Swedish archbishop Nathan Söderblom charged Schantz with improving the living conditions on the island. He tried his best, though his schemes were not always successful. His imported ram got loose and killed three indigenous rams in one day, and the bull calf descended from his imported cow took to jumping fences like a deer. He did, however, build rails for bringing the boats up on land, and imported small boat engines and guns, bought by the islanders with the help of microcredit loans from a charitable society. At that time, Schantz noted, Runö and the entire Estonian Swedish population were popular causes in Sweden.

In 1928 the island harvest failed following long rains, and starvation threatened. Schantz campaigned for food aid with the help of a friendly newspaper editor, and at the end of November a ship arrived. On board was a group of Swedish "Runö friends," with sacks of rye and wheat, seed potatoes, sugar, paraffin, herrings, and other groceries, as well as a Christmas present for each home, containing coffee, biscuits, and sweets. Hunger abated, and improvements continued. In the liberal and democratic 1920s development was everywhere. Schantz noted how the Swedish Birkas school, in Pürksi, and the new Estonian Swedish journal *Kustbon* (established 1917) were spreading new and modern ideas. On Runö, a farmer built a small plant to process seal blubber. The farmer's son started the first grocery shop on the island, selling fabrics, sowing tools, paper and envelopes, and candy. Schantz himself initiated a land shift, since the fields were small, narrow strips of land. Development continued after his departure in 1930, including a healthcare centre run by a Swedish nurse, and visits by a Swedish agronomist who taught the farmers how to further improve the land.

The future looked so bright. They didn't know it then, but they were running out of time. In 1934 President Konstantin Päts staged a nationalist coup, in order to subvert the right-wing League of Veterans of the Estonian War of Independence (the Vaps movement), from gaining power. The country ceased to be a democracy, though it was not a repressive dictatorship either. Päts did, however, implement a policy of Estonianising the country, a milder variant of the harsh Russification measures of the 1880s. Minority schools, journals, and societies were curtailed. Schools had to teach in Estonian, and minority children were not allowed to speak their own languages on school premises. The "era of silence" ended with the 1938 election and a new constitution reducing the power of the presidency.

In the summer of 1939, Estonia was forced into a Soviet "mutual assistance pact," following the secret protocol of the Molotov-Ribbentrop Pact. The treaty, the existence of which was always denied by the Soviet Union, was signed on 23 August 1939. It planned the partition of eastern Europe into Russian and German spheres of interest. Poland was to be divided. Finland, Estonia, Latvia, and most of Lithuania and Romania were assigned to the Soviet sphere of interest, and the rest of Lithuania and most of Poland to Nazi Germany. Within weeks, Poland was invaded, first by Germany from the west, and then by Russia from the east.

Kustbon, the Estonian Swedish weekly journal, reported that fateful summer on the "new agreement" between Estonia and the Soviet Union, whereby Estonia would allow Soviet military bases in return for keeping the peace agreement of 1920 and the nonaggression pact of 1932. Two weeks later the journal was devoted to the sensational news that Hitler had called the Baltic Germans back to Germany, the Heim ins Reich policy of persuading ethnic Germans around the world to come back to the homeland. Many Baltic Germans had already left after the First World War. Now fourteen thousand people, almost all the Germans who had remained in Estonia, left the country in the following months. Most of their families had lived in Estonia since the twelfth and thirteenth centuries. They left their ancestral homes, their grand estates, their town houses and professions, perhaps because they were Nazi sympathisers or German nationalists believing in the pan-Germanic ideal, but probably also because they were wary of the Soviet Union. For the Nazis, calling Germans home and settling them in the occupied territories was a deliberate colonising policy. The intention was to create a Greater Germany, with *lebensraum* and opportunities for all ethnic Germans, cleansed of Jews, and supported by a subhuman labour reservoir of Slavic people. Most of the Baltic Germans were resettled in Poland, in expropriated farms and houses whose owners had been expelled to make way for them. More than a million Germans, some Baltic, others from Germany itself, others again from German colonies in eastern Europe and the rest of the world, settled in Poland during the war.

After the war there was a mass expulsion of millions of ethnic Germans from eastern Europe, mainly from Poland, parts of the Soviet Union, and Czechoslovakia. Many people fled before they were expelled and evacuated, to escape from the violent revenge of the Red Army. Russian officers had little sympathy for German civilians who had supported a regime that caused the deaths of millions of Russians, and allowed the soldiers a free hand. Rape was a weapon of war, then as it is now. Hundreds of thousands of German refugees died in the chaos of the flight, freezing to death in the snow, bombed, and attacked by aerial machine-gun fire.

In Estonia in 1939 the same issue of *Kustbon* also carried a short article entitled "No Cause for Nervousness," about the movements of Russian troops in Estonia. It ended, memorably: "In the areas where Russian troops will be stationed it is rumoured that local people may be forced to evacuate their farms, leave their belongings, or even have their property confiscated. No one needs to fear anything like that." Less than a year later, in June 1940, the people of the islands of Odensholm, Rågö, and Nargö, most of them Swedish, were forced to evacuate, in order to make space for Soviet military bases. A year later, on 16 June 1940, Latvia and Estonia received ultimatums from the Soviet Union. Both countries, following the course of Lithuania, capitulated. Two days after that, Estonia was an occupied country. The NKVD, precursor of the KGB, entered Estonia together with Red Army units, and the arrests and deportations began.

On 21 June 1940 a popular uprising was staged in order to establish a puppet government. A 1987 Estonian book gives the Soviet version of events, quoting from contemporary newspapers:

> Sirens rang out almost simultaneously at 9 o'clock in the morning from Tallinn's biggest factories and plants. It was a signal for the workers to take action. Crowds were gathering at the workers' sportshall on the Pärnu highway, forming columns of people . . . "We don't need policemen! We'll establish order ourselves," the workers shouted. The policemen who had just arrived at the square retreated. And the Estonian workers proved that they were not a motley group of people torn by internal contradictions but a united front, as strong as steel, welded together by common desires and ideas. The meeting was held in an orderly fashion. The crowd of thirty or forty thousand people gave their full endorsement to the speeches and resolutions made in Freedom Square.

The formal annexation of Estonia took place in August 1940. Soon all non-Soviet public activity was proscribed. Soviet soldiers emptied the stores because of the artificially low exchange rate and the shortages in Russia. Banks, businesses, factories, and workshops with more than ten workers were nationalised. Houses larger than two hundred square meters could be expropriated. Bank accounts exceeding 2,000 kroons (about £200) were frozen, along with the contents of all safes. Leaving work without permission was punishable by jail.

On 30 July 1940 President Konstantin Päts, whose grandson Matti I met in 1991, was deported to Leningrad and subsequently to Ufa, the capital of the Soviet Republic of Bashkortostan in the Ural Mountains, together with his son, his daughter-in-law, and his two grandsons. A year later he was rearrested and sent to prison, accused of counter-revolutionary sabotage and anti-Soviet and counter-revolutionary propaganda and agitation. In 1952 a series of psychiatric hospitalizations began: in one of the more tragic Soviet ironies of the time, he was diagnosed as mentally ill because of his persistent belief that he was the president of Estonia. In 1954 he was briefly detained in a hospital in Estonia, but recognition by hospital staff (former subjects encouraging his "delusions") meant that he was once again removed, to the Burashevo Mental Hospital in the Kalinin region, where he died in 1956.

Almost all Estonian politicians from the independence era fled, committed suicide, or were deported. The NKVD arrested about three hundred people a month, mainly those regarded as opposed to the occupation, until 14 June 1941, six days before the Nazi invasion of the Soviet Union, when thousands of Estonians, Latvians, and Lithuanians, most of them from professional backgrounds, were deported in one night. Families were broken up, the men sent to labour camps, and the majority of the women and children to Siberian collective farms. That summer, 230 Estonian officers serving in the Red Army were also arrested. As the army retreated, they forced thousands of men to retreat with them—in all some twenty-five thousand people voluntarily or involuntarily evacuated to the Soviet Union in the summer of 1941. About three thousand men died on the way, before they reached their final destination.

The intellectual elite of the country was being decimated. Soon libraries, archives, and all publishing was under Soviet control. The Museum of Occupations in Tallinn, which opened in 2003, has published research on Estonian Soviet censorship. In the summer of 1940, following the occupation, more than two hundred newspapers and journals were banned by a resolution of the chief of internal affairs. Twenty-nine authors were banned outright. All exchanges with foreign journals were prohibited, and foreign literature could no longer be imported.

A new regulation was issued in August that year. All literature containing anti-Soviet "slander and agitation," and all literature justifying "bourgeois exploitation," or inciting "chauvinistic anger and hostility," along with all theological literature, was to be removed from libraries. In south Estonia the books were sent to Tartu University Library, where they were destroyed. In north Estonia they were sent to the State Library in Tallinn, where they were preserved.

That month lists of banned books and publications were compiled. The first list contained 130 works in Russian. The second contained memoirs and other biographical works in Estonian, fiction and children's books. The third specified magazines, monographs, brochures, manuals, and all books published by particular publishing houses. The fourth included Russian and other foreign books, and covered such subjects as journalism, theology, education, politics, philosophy, and history. There was a further list of 111 banned plays, and a list of books that were partly banned, mainly textbooks, that could still be used for the time being. These lists were made public.

One particular list was kept secret. More than a hundred children's books were on it, and many works in Russian. Altogether, according to the museum, more than fifteen hundred books were banned. The censored books were removed from libraries, bookshops, and publishing houses, and shredded or burnt.

By September old textbooks and reference works used in schools were banned. Circulars were issued to school boards and head teachers to warn them that "reactionary literature," literature "justifying and supporting capitalist exploitation," and "anti-Soviet and anti-communist literature" must be removed from school libraries. Later, works by communists who had already been purged, like Grigory Zinoviev, Leon Trotsky, and Nikolai Bukharin, were also banned.

That month the Publishing Centre of the Estonian SSR was launched. It was responsible for the management and inspection of publishing activities and bookshops. The Soviet Estonian *Glavlit* (the Main Administration for Literary and Publishing Affairs) was founded in 1940 to "review" all books. At the end of 1940 libraries of independent societies and associations were banned, and independent-minded librarians everywhere were replaced by "loyal citizens." All in all, probably some two hundred thousand books were destroyed in the first occupation, including seventy thousand volumes of theology belonging to Tartu University.

During the Nazi occupation (1941–44) censorship continued. The Nazis made their own lists of banned books, compiled anonymously and kept secret. The first one was ready in November 1941, and banned seven categories of books: Soviet Russian literature from 1917 to 1941 (except science and classics without communist commentaries), all communist literature, English and French literature from 1933 in the original and in translation (except new editions of classics), Estonian literature published in 1940/41 (except purely scientific works), Jewish literature in all languages, works by non-Jews having emigrated from Germany since 1933, and "anti-German" literature in all languages. The list contained 197 completely banned authors, (only 16 were Estonian).

A second list banned individual books and periodicals, and all works issued by certain publishing houses. Textbooks had to be approved. Some works, for example on sexuality, or analyses of totalitarianism, were banned by both the Soviet and Nazi censors.

The returning Soviet occupying force carried on the censorship and destruction of books. According to the museum, the entire Tallinn Central Library, containing some 150,000 volumes, including the archives of Estonian literature, was destroyed between 1946 and 1950. Independent publishing was ruined, and the libraries of Estonia were decimated by the removal and destruction of books. From June 1945 all typewriters required registration, and publishers (those few who had survived the war and deportations) needed to show an "unblemished political past." By now, a quarter of all books being published were "sociopolitical." Finally, in 1949, most foreign literature in libraries was destroyed. Foreign books from the State Library were shredded. Lists of permitted foreign literature were created, containing 109 classical authors. In 1950 much of Soviet Estonian literature was purged and banned. By 1952 almost everything that had been published during independence was banned and destroyed. And Estonia, of course, was only a small country. Both the Soviet Union and Nazi Germany did more or less the same things in all the countries they occupied, working diligently, following their meticulous plans for censorship and repression.

After Stalin's death in 1953, Nikita Khrushchev began preparations for what became known as the thaw, the era of liberalisation, which ended in a coup in 1964. During Khrushchev's period of power, Soviet censorship was loosened, culminating in the publication in 1962 of Aleksandr Solzhenitsyn's novella *One Day in the Life of Ivan Denisovich* in the literary magazine *Novy Mir*, edited by Aleksandr Tvardovsky. It was the first text about the Gulag published in the Soviet Union, and it was personally approved by Khrushchev.

After the 1964 coup, the long era of stagnation began, led by Leonid Brezhnev until his death in 1982. The 1965–66 show trial of the writers Andrei Sinyavsky and Yuli Daniel—accused of anti-Soviet agitation and propaganda, having published anti-Soviet editorials abroad under pseudonyms—symbolised the hardening climate. They were sentenced to seven and five years respectively, in strict-regime labour camps. Then Solzhenitsyn was accused of not following Soviet principles in 1968, and was eventually arrested and deported in 1974.

I am thinking again about Toivo and Inna's books. The books they owned, by Balzac, Galsworthy, Hardy, Shaw, Zola, Maupassant, and London, were passed by the Soviet censors, and encouraged by the authorities. The themes of poverty, greed, and corruption under capitalism were welcome, of course. In 1987 Gorbachev's *glasnost* and *perestroika*, openness and reform, had started in earnest. A commission was established to return previously banned books to the main library catalogues. But Nabokov's *Lolita*, which Toivo and Inna also had on their shelves, was the real test of the end of censorship. Trying to find out when the first Estonian edition was published, I found a copy of it for sale on eBay. Described as a "rare first edition," it was published in 1990, thirty-five years after the first edition was published, in Paris, in 1955. And how did Toivo and Inna come to have this strange and pivotal book, this still controversial literary masterpiece, in their modest library? I don't know. But I think Toivo may have bought it. He had a wider horizon somewhere inside him, beyond his alcoholic demons.

After the Soviet invasion, the Estonian Swedish journal *Kustbon* duly became a Soviet organ. The 1940 showcase elections were reported on the first page on 20 July, under the heading "Exceptional Participation in Parliamentary Elections." The article stated that each farm must acquire a Soviet flag, for which precise dimensions were given. Almost as an afterthought, it also informed readers that all bank assets had been frozen until further notice. The issue also carried a critical article about the previous government's treatment of minorities, with examples of post-1934 laws restricting their rights. Despite the obvious political caution of the editors, the Soviet authorities still closed *Kustbon* down.

In October 1940 the first issue of its replacement, the Swedish *Sovjet-Estland* (*Soviet Estonia*), was published. "The 21 June this year was a great day of freedom for the Estonian proletariat," the editors proclaimed on the first page.

The first rays of socialism dawned over our land. Step by step the working class has battled to vanquish the violence of the capitalists. Now, power is in the firm hands of the working people. Justice, equality, and socialism are the slogans for our class-conscious workers and farmers. Soviet Estonia has new, unlimited and wide possibilities for development. The walls that imprisoned the minorities in this land have fallen. All are now one people, and all minorities can live their lives within the boundaries of our great country. Cooperation with other people in our country has become possible for our minorities. Our working people's government, and our leader the Estonian Communist Party, has shown its goodwill towards the working Swedish-speaking people's struggles and wishes, and intends to see to the well-being of the Swedish-speaking coastal people. A step in the right direction has been made by giving them their own Swedish newspaper. This newspaper will come out once a week under the name of *Sovjet-Estland* ... *Sovjet-Estland* wishes to be the leader and guide to correct socialist-communist basic thought. With our Leninist Stalinist basic philosophy we begin our work, and strive to be worthy workers, building socialism. All those who want to work for our country's well-being must mobilise around *Sovjet-Estland* and help with its distribution in their area. We are ready for our great task.

The Editors

In articles on the inside pages the Estonian Swedes were encouraged to "work in a socialist way," to "follow work programs with honour, to increase work productivity, to develop our socialist industry, to raise our socialist culture, in order to quickly catch up with the other free people of the great Soviet Union and to build socialist society." "Together with the working people of the entire Soviet Union the working people of the Soviet Estonian Socialist Republic will freely celebrate the twenty-third birthday of the great October Revolution. Under the leadership of the Communist Bolshevik Party the working people of the Soviet Estonian Socialist republic have begun building a new, free, and happy life, exterminating capitalists and landowners." Improving the "sanitary conditions" and the "socialist culture" (such as it was) of the Estonian Swedes was also on the agenda. The rest of the newspaper was mostly about the difficulties in Europe: "pea rationing in Finland," "shortage of meat in Denmark," "the dictatorship in France," "the Nazification of Norway," "the catastrophic situation for Swedish farmers." And "great progress of coal production in the Soviet Union."

A hasty provisional land reform followed. In Läänemaa, the county of the northwest coastal region that included Noarootsi, it was reported that 1,764 new farms were being created. *Sovjet-Estland* described the local land redistribution. Some of the Swedes, the reporter wrote, still "waited for help from the old fatherland [Sweden], despite the fact that they knew that even there the working people suffered under the yoke of the capitalists. After the 21st of June the atmosphere was transformed in Rikull. Still, not everybody was happy. Even amongst the Swedish minority there are backwards, politically ignorant people who can't find their place in the new society."

The journalist meets an elderly woman:

"Well, I wanted some land," she says. "Not for me, but I have two sons. For two years they were away, but now they've come back."

"But you wanted to move to Sweden, too, to your sons. So now they are back and you have changed your plans?"

"I cried with happiness when they came back," says the old woman, and dries her eyes on her apron. "And if we get land they won't need to [go]. Then they could stay at home."

"Home?" the journalist writes. "Even though the old woman was Swedish, she didn't want to leave Estonia, her home. It's not easy to leave your motherland, to leave the soil that your ancestors have cultivated. The soil is barren and stony, and yet you love it.

It is the soil of the motherland. It is impossible to replant an old tree—it will languish. Those who propagate for the removal to the 'old motherland' should remember that."

Within four years most of the Swedes were gone from Estonia, probably including this journalist. Who remembers now that hasty land reform, wiped out by the collectivisation a few years later?

During the early part of the first Soviet occupation, Birkas school was occupied by Russian troops. After much negotiation Fridolf Isberg, acting headmaster, managed to reopen the school, which was in a bad state after the troop occupations. They still thought they could carry on. The curriculum was changed, replacing geography, history, and Estonian with Russian language and the mandatory study of the 1936 constitution, also known as the "Stalin Constitution." I find it online. There was much to study: thirteen chapters, 146 articles, guaranteeing civil rights and gender equality, all subject, of course, to Article 3:

> In the U.S.S.R. all power belongs to the working people of town and country as represented by the Soviets of Working People's Deputies.

Article 118 of Stalin's constitution outlined the right to work:

> Citizens of the U.S.S.R. have the right to work, that is, are guaranteed the right to employment and payment for their work in accordance with its quantity and quality. The right to work is ensured by the socialist organization of the national economy, the steady growth of the productive forces of Soviet society, the elimination of the possibility of economic crises, and the abolition of unemployment.

Work is not only a right, however, it is also a duty, defined by Article 12:

In the U.S.S.R. work is a duty and a matter of honor for every able-bodied citizen, in accordance with the principle: "He who does not work, neither shall he eat." The principle applied in the U.S.S.R. is that of socialism: "From each according to his ability, to each according to his work."

I am slightly startled by this phrase—it doesn't look right. And it is, in fact, a reformulation of Karl Marx's famous phrase "From *each according to his ability, to each according to his need*," taken from his tract criticising the German Social Democratic Gotha Program of 1875. That phrase came to be seen in the Soviet Union as a defining description of communism (the goal), rather than of socialism (the reality, later described as "actually existing socialism"), so they rewrote it. From each according to his ability, to each according to his work. It seems oddly capitalist. I am reminded of George Orwell, and the post-revolutionary anthem in *Animal Farm*:

> *For that day we all must labour,*
> *Though we die before it break;*
> *Cows and horses, geese and turkeys,*
> *All must toil for freedom's sake.*

The school's model farm, meanwhile, was transformed into a *sovkhoz* (state-owned farm), and a five-year plan was drawn up. All religious literature from the library was sent to Tallinn, according to the new censorship rules, and a "red corner" was established in the common room, with Soviet slogans, and portraits of Marx, Engels, Lenin, and Stalin on red paper. A year later the accountant and one of the teachers were deported.

On 22 June 1941, a year after the Soviet invasion, Operation Barbarossa, the German invasion of the Soviet Union, began. On 5 July the *Wehrmacht* forces reached Estonia. Some thirty-five thousand people voluntarily joined the Red Army, and a further thirty-three thousand were conscripted. A similar number joined the other side. The country, and sometimes even individual families, Swedes as well as Estonians, were divided between Communist and Nazi sympathisers, the liberal centre attacked from both sides. Nazi Germany prevailed, and Estonia was added to the *Reichskommissariat Ostland,* the new German eastern provinces. A Nazi directorate was put in place, and the work to make Estonia *Judenrein* ("clean of Jews"), the primary goal in occupied countries, began.

Jews did not live freely in the Russian Empire. They were largely confined to the Pale of Settlement, roughly the area formerly comprising the old Polish-Lithuanian Commonwealth, present-day Lithuania, Belarus, Poland, Moldova, Ukraine, and parts of western Russia. Even within the Pale, they were not allowed to live in certain cities. Jews had not been allowed to settle in Estonia until the end of the nineteenth century. Hence before the war there were only some forty-three hundred Jews in Estonia, about half of whom lived in Tallinn.

There was a great deal of cultural autonomy for all minorities up until 1934. Anti-Semitic materials were banned after independence, and continued to be banned under President Konstantin Päts's mildly authoritarian regime. Nazism as a political movement was outlawed. Despite the fact that the community was so small, there was a Jewish representative of parliament, a Zionist youth movement, Yiddish newspapers, and a chair of Jewish studies at Tartu. All were destroyed after the German invasion.

Two weeks after the invasion, the *Omakaitse,* the Estonian territorial army in Nazi service, started searching for hidden Jews. Most Jews had, by then, already escaped to Russia. The ones who remained were virtually all killed: only twelve Estonian Jews are known to have survived the Holocaust in Estonia, fewer than in any other country occupied by the Nazis.

The Germans occupied Estonia for four years, from 1941 to 1944. In that time at least fifteen thousand Soviet prisoners of war were killed as slave labourers in Estonia, worked to death in camps. Alongside Estonian Jews, thousands of Jews from other occupied countries were transported to be killed in Estonia—at Kalevi-Liiva, at Vaivara, at Klooga, and other places—along with hundreds of Roma people. Some six thousand ethnic Estonians, and another thousand people described as being of 'uncertain nationality', were also killed by the Nazis.

Some Estonians tried to help the Jews, notably Uku Masing, a linguist and philosopher who was awarded the Righteous Among the Nations honorific by Yad Vashem and the Israeli Supreme Court. Masing, an extraordinarily gifted man, and an expert on Semitic languages, saved the life of a friend, Isidor Levin, at great personal risk.

And the Estonian Swedes? For them, not much changed at first. At Birkas, the curriculum of the school was altered once more, German replacing Russian and the study of the Stalin constitution. In 1943, however, the German army began to mobilise men from the Swedish-speaking community as well as from the Estonian one. The illegal flights to Sweden—which had been going on since the beginning of the war—increased dramatically then. Families, Estonian as well as Swedish, fled in small fishing boats, risking the twin dangers of the Baltic Sea and discovery by German military patrols.

In February 1944 the Red Army began its advance towards Tallinn. In March it bombed the city, and tens of thousands of people fled. Some ended up in displaced people's camps in Germany after the war. Some were shot, either by German or by Russian troops. Some who had fought with the Germans, or collaborated, fled to the forests in 1944, joining the anti-Soviet partisans. The Forest Brothers, active in Latvia and Lithuania as well, kept up a losing guerrilla war against the Soviet occupation long after the war, fading into a dismal existence in hiding. Soviet propaganda portrayed them as Nazi sympathisers. Swedish, American, and British secret services helped the Forest Brothers after the war, but in the end many guerrilla units were destroyed by the actions of the British spy Kim Philby, who gave MI6 information about them to the KGB. The last Forest Brother in Estonia, August Sabbe, was discovered in 1978 by a river near his former home. He drowned, possibly committing suicide, before he could be arrested.

Collectivisation in Estonia took place in 1949. Stalin planned a preemptive mass deportation from the western borderlands beforehand, in order to weaken opposition: on 25–26 March 1949, 20,700 Estonians, mainly from the countryside, were deported. "Kulaks," "collaborators," and "nationalists" were the main targets. Lists were drawn up, and people were arrested and sent off to the Gulag. Few came back. All but one of the collective farms on the peninsula of Noarootsi was founded in the month after the deportations. The last one, Freedom (formerly the village of Harga), was established on 30 April 1949. The thirty-two villages on the peninsula were turned into twenty-three collective farms. Each village formerly had a Swedish and an Estonian name. The collective farms were given Soviet Estonian names: Lenin, Red Flag, Victory, Red Dawn, Hero, Red Star, New Life, Forward, New Way, Partisan, Kalinin, and so on.

Almost all the Swedes had left by then, half the inhabitants on the peninsula. Some of their farms had been taken over by Estonians from Russia, resettled by the Germans. Those Estonians had little in common with the farmers and villagers on Noarootsi. They had grown up with the revolution and didn't know how to live thriftily, which was essential on that poor soil, where everything was recycled over and over. The newcomers had no such traditions, and probably no genuine hope of staying or commitment to the new farms. People said that they burnt furniture and boats for firewood, and that they didn't take care of the animals. Overall Estonian agricultural production declined dramatically—the effect of collectivisation everywhere.

*   *   *

In 1950, 1951, and 1952 the small collective farms amalgamated, finally leaving only Lenin and Kalinin on the peninsula. By now the tensions between the newcomers and the original inhabitants had subsided, submerged in the cultural tidal wave of collectivisation. Collective farm centres like Pürksi were planned centrally, and were more or less the same all over the Soviet Union, with their collective dining rooms, cultural programmes, schools, and childcare. After a few years, collective farmworkers were paid small salaries—in the beginning they had to work for food, like in the feudal era. "He who does not work, neither shall he eat." In 1965 Kalinin on the peninsula and Kirov on the mainland merged into Sutlepa Kolhoos, headquartered on the mainland. In 1976 Sutlepa merged with Lenin, covering most of the peninsula and a strip of land on the mainland. Inevitably, Lenin was the first and the last. It was renamed the Noarootsi Kolhoos in 1990 and closed, finally, in 1993.

SEVEN

Dear Comrades

When I was doing my fieldwork I was not as yet aware of most of the history I have just described. Not all of it was accessible yet—President Lennart Meri set up the Estonian International Commission for Investigation of Crimes Against Humanity in 1998, which was succeeded in 2008 by the Estonian Institute of Historical Memory, established by President Toomas Ilves. The Museum of Occupations opened in 2003. Much of the history was still largely unknown in 1993–94. I visited the historical archives in Tallinn to see what I could find. It was empty and quiet. A pale librarian tried half-heartedly to help me, but the place was still Soviet enough to make it a difficult process, and my Estonian was not good enough to make sense of what I read.

That same day I went on to Rocca-al-Mare, the Estonian Open Air Museum, outside Tallinn. Soviet guides, apparently, used to tell tourists that the poor nineteenth-century wooden huts and houses were how all rural Estonians lived before the Soviet liberation, ignoring the 1920 land reform, and twenty years of thriving independent farming. Now, the museum was busy with women and children selling crafts to the few tourists. Farther away from the entrance, hidden by the old peasant dwellings, impoverished people were selling their own belongings to the few tourists coming by: cutlery and plates, cheap sweaters, old vases and lamps.

Seeing it, I remembered St. Petersburg. I had been there two years previously, in the autumn of 1991, and wandered through the market with a Russian friend. Men and women were sitting on the street and pavement, bleakly, quietly, selling what they could. A man, his feet wrapped in rags, sat in front of a small pile of rusty nails. Next to him a man was selling small fish the Neva River, four or five of them on a cracked plate. A woman nearby was selling some broken plates. My friend walked past in silence, her pockets crammed with the contents of the minibar, and all the soap and shampoo, from my hotel room. We were walking back to her family's flat, a relatively privileged few rooms from a subdivided pre-war building. She gave me tea made from water filtered, boiled, and frozen, to purify it.

By October it was getting cold in Estonia. Tiina, the new teacher who had lived in Denmark for a year, affected not to understand why the school was so cold, or why Toivo and Inna's flat, where she visited me, was so cold. I looked at her in disbelief, and she hastily changed the subject.

By now I was writing long reports, divided into tentative quasi-anthropological headings: "Displacement, Comprehension, Production," "Sanity and Representativeness," "Gender," "Inside/Outside," "The Material Culture of the Home," "Silence and Distance," "Transience and the Extraordinary Variety of Breakfasts." I analysed every conversation, and wrote long field notes. But sometimes the depth confused the surface. "Don't drink that cold water," Toivo would often say, commenting, I thought, on how much water I drank, and the difference in patterns of consumption between us. The Estonians seemed to drink nothing but coffee, tea, and alcohol. You could build an argument on a comment like that—in fact I think I probably did. Later, I found out that the kitchen water had been condemned as "not of drinking quality." Toivo and Inna didn't quite want to say, but nor did they really want me to be poisoned.

*   *   *

Toivo got drunk on a regular basis, a periodical drinker. When he wasn't drunk he was unhappy, wandering between the kitchen and the living room, sighing deeply, his suffering so ostentatious, and yet so existential. One drunk night he showed me his military diary, a tiny notebook filled with drawings and poems. There was an Estonian flag, crossed with a whip and a spiked club. *Got uns Mit* [*God with Us*], he had scribbled under it in broken German. To the right was an eagle—Russia—with blood dripping from its outstretched claw, beak open in an imagined hiss. There were American cars, women dancing with a devil grinning in the foreground, the legs of dancing people, and, sadly, a bottle crossed out. His friends teased him, he slurred, looking at me intently, about having a "beautiful woman" living with him, "a second wife." He professed to love me as a "brother" and not a "husband," but he hovered uncomfortably near me, both physically and mentally. Inna was away again—she left, usually with the children, when he drank, leaving me alone with him.

Sometimes they tried to entertain me together. One such evening I remember because they got their old photo albums out. His were mostly from his time in the army in Novosibirsk in 1968–70: small snapshots with a brownish tint. Military service was supposed to be "an honorable duty of Soviet citizens." An honorable duty with brutal, sometimes fatal, bullying in the ranks, directed against most minorities. The Estonians stuck together in the army. The photos in the albums were mostly staged jokes sent back to his mother, of his head sticking up from the sand, or flying through the air, looking like a tougher blond Elvis, with sunglasses and long sideburns. There was one photo of Toivo sitting with his friends on a bench in front of a concrete block on the sand, looking at a small bag of nuts from Sweden, part of some relatives' food parcel. I looked at the Swedish peanuts—the packaging was comforting, a familiar sign, even in that black-and-white snapshot from so long ago.

At about this time I had an accident with my car, driving over a stone on the road, two hours from the collective farm. The car ground to a halt, and I was stuck, with the hitchhiking kids I had picked up some miles back. We sat around waiting until a car with three men stopped. They examined my car for at least half an hour, leisurely discussing what might be wrong, trying to extract, with some difficulties, the precise details of the accident. Then a car mechanic from Haapsalu stopped his lorry to help, too. The men continued to worry over the engine, and finally decided that they would tow the car, with one of the men, rather than me, behind the wheel. "The power brakes don't work so well when the engine is turned off," one of them explained kindly, "but don't worry, he is a good driver." The children and I climbed into the lorry, and the other men followed. We drove to Risti, the nearest town, where the mechanic knew the local policeman, a Russian, but nevertheless deemed a decent enough guardian of the car whilst arrangements could be made.

The policeman, holding a mangy growling Alsatian on a rope, agreed to keep the car in his yard. The men proceeded to discuss the precise location of where it should be parked in the yard, in surreal detail. The children, used to waiting, lounged about, as did I, by now barely a participant in my own fate. The position finally agreed, the parking done, the men suddenly left with the children, leaving me barely enough time even to thank them. They had already arranged with the mechanic that he would drive me home, a detour of some fifty kilometers.

It turned out, as we chatted in his cab, that the mechanic's mother was Swedish, though he himself didn't speak the language. He came with me into the flat, and he and Toivo had an intense and prolonged consultation. Toivo told me to go and wait in the kitchen, and I did, by now exhausted and somewhat emotional. Erki came in, and asked in his hoarse and monotone English (I taught him) what had happened. I told him, voice unsteady. He didn't say anything, standing by the sink, looking down, thumbing the cheap fake wood surround, his presence comforting nevertheless. Toivo and the mechanic returned, having settled on a plan, and had some coffee in the kitchen. The mechanic left, as suddenly as the others, refusing any payment before I had even offered it, Toivo nodding sagely in the background.

Soon my car became a concern of the whole village. Kulla's daughter in Tallinn was roped in, because she had so many "contacts," knew so many "young men," in Tallinn. At two she rang, saying that the car would have to be towed to the Tallinn Volvo centre. She said she would ring and get a price for the repair, and would call me back. I said not to worry, they couldn't know the price before seeing the car, and she agreed half-heartedly. Toivo would have to arrange it with the school, she said, shouting on the crackly line that she would call me again "if she had any news." Toivo rang Laine, who rang four people to see if they could take me, towing the car, and, finally, offered me the help of the school driver. I said I would pay for the petrol. She made an airy gesture, and said, "How nice of you, but don't let us speak of such things." Then she looked at me meaningfully and said that if I didn't like it in this family she could find me another one, or I could move back to the hotel. She knew, of course, about Toivo's drinking, but she wasn't going to mention it.

I should have moved out there and then: nothing good could have come of staying, particularly not for my hosts, as would soon become obvious. The car incident delayed the move, because I felt so well cared for afterwards. A short time later I accidentally set fire to the kitchen in the flat, forgetting to switch off the nonautomatic electric kettle. I had put the kettle on for tea and forgot all about it, reading in my room. Toivo and a friend arrived home, drunk, to smoke and smouldering lino. They shouted, and threw water on the flames. I ran out into an arena of two silhouetted men moving through the smoke, coughing. Soon the fire was out, the floor wet and charred.

Inna was away, but got back shortly afterwards. She was very calm. "*Juhtus*," she said soothingly, "it happens." I was deeply upset. Neither Inna nor Toivo seemed to mind at all, and seemed, in fact, mildly puzzled by my emotion. I wonder now if their lack of recrimination, their instant forgiveness, came about because Inna felt guilty about the high rent she was charging me, or ashamed, perhaps, of Toivo's bouts of drinking and her own regular absences. But they were also essentially kind people, and they didn't want me to feel bad. In the end, though, I think also that the fire genuinely didn't matter much to them. They seemed surprised by how upset and remorseful I was. The lino was scarred, and I bought a rug to cover it. The kettle was ruined, and I replaced it. They probably didn't see the scarred lino again until they packed up the flat and moved on several years later. I got a reputation for being accident-prone, which amused them, and we all carried on.

There was something liberating about their attitude towards material goods—they did not identify themselves with anything they owned. They did not think of others in terms of what they owned. Everyone on the collective farm owned not only roughly the same amount of things, but actually more or less exactly the same things. I thought then that perhaps we care too much about our belongings, our cleanliness, our fussy and fastidious material arrangements. Maybe something really is lost—time, and solidarity—in our obsession with material goods, our trap of savings, loans, and debts, our caring for the endless things that we collect along the way.

The accident and the fire broke down a barrier between us, however, and in the long run that was not helpful. My second report to my supervisor ended on a bleak note: "Since I started this report the situation in my family has become untenable, and I am about to start the process of finding a new family, which is rather daunting and difficult. The alcoholism of the father makes it impossible for me to stay, since I haven't been able to re-build the barrier between us [since the fire], and he is becoming threatening when drunk, especially when his wife is not here. I lock my door at night, and hear him pacing up and down, talking to himself, putting the radio on full blast, muttering angrily." I ended, with slightly pathetic bravura: "It makes me realise that issues about self-reflexivity are essentially experiential questions, which you are bound to come up against in the field, but which there doesn't seem much point in spending much time on before you go. Hoping to hear from you soon."

My supervisor wrote back, cutting to the chase: "The issue of your sexuality is clearly the most difficult issue of all. Honorary man is the best hope. I was able to be honorary woman in Trinidad which worked very well. Much as I want to see your work progress," he added, "your safety and welfare come first and therefore do not hesitate to shift your ground or even move field site if you think you are in any danger at all. It's just not worth it."

I didn't think I was in danger, but honorary man? The best I might hope for was honorary (accident-prone) child, and even that was quite hard to maintain. I suspect that the transition from man to honorary woman is generally easier than that from woman to honorary man. But perhaps, also, when you do fieldwork in a culture so similar to your own it's less easy to conceal your identity. Much as I knew them, I think now, they also knew me.

I had to replace my car whilst it was being repaired, and eventually found a "contact" via Riima, my journalist friend in Tallinn, to help. He took me to the second-hand car market in Mustamäe, a huge repository of second-hand Western cars replacing the eastwards-drifting Ladas.

"I can say that the Russian market is such a big hole for the Ladas," he said in English as we wandered around the huge market, my feet like blocks of ice. A Lada in St. Petersburg cost $500 more than in Tallinn—they liked Ladas because they could get parts. "They think it's normal," he said, "to have such a battle with the car."

"It must have been strange," I said, tired, "when all the Western cars started to come into Estonia."

"Why?" he said sternly, looking at me intently. The young and business-minded didn't want to be reminded of the past.

I found, eventually, a little Renault that seemed all right, though in fact it was a failure from the beginning. I had several hitchhikers with me as I drove back to the peninsula the following day, some of whom were my students, and a Russian woman I didn't know. They sat in thoughtful silence as the car inexplicably ground to a halt, time and time again. I have no memory of what I did with that clapped-out old car, but I know I eventually got my Volvo back, with a brand-new engine from the Volvo centre. But in the depths of winter it wouldn't start—in the deepest cold, when the collective farm Ladas started easily, my Volvo was dead. The men would gather around it, hood open, to help me start it. There they stood, without gloves or hats, leisurely discussing the internal workings of the Volvo, whilst I stood with them, nearly weeping with the numbing cold of minus 30 degrees. And the guilt of being helped by people who expected nothing in return.

On that trip back from Tallinn we made it—just—in time for me to join the new aerobic class in school. The class, attended by teenage girls, was surprisingly lenient. The most taxing exercise was a fast walk in a circle to very loud music. The rest of it consisted of leisurely stretches—circling the wrists and ankles and so on—to encouraging and entirely superfluous shouts from our tracksuited and trim instructor, whom I had never seen before. I only went once, and I don't think it continued, in any case. Winter eventually ended most extracurricular activities. Life became increasingly routine, circumscribed by the cold and the dark, and a kind of winter fatigue that affected everyone. I recorded a grim succession of days in my diary, including a record of the food we ate, because I was always mildly hungry. Thus I know that on 15 November 1993 I had stale bread with cheese for breakfast, and that I then went for a walk, though I felt too tired to go all the way to Österby, the nearest village. I washed a sheet in the bucket, and picked up my post. School lunch was cabbage soup and dry bread. I corrected the horrifyingly bad English tests. Dinner was buckwheat with little bits of meat. The snow, I wrote, was drifting like dry white dust across the roads, and it got dark by three in the afternoon. At night the temperature dropped to minus 15 degrees. The following day I walked in the hazy afternoon, the sun setting across the fields, trees frosted and wintry. Everything was blissfully quiet. I was tired, and often hungry, but even now, twenty years later, I miss those long quiet walks in that melancholy and restful landscape.

At about this time Toivo, Inna, and Kulla invited Katarina and me to come to the beach resort of Pärnu, to stay with some friends of theirs. Pärnu was once a pretty spa resort, but in the early 1990s, and off-season, it was run-down and depressing. The friends invited us out to dinner and a "variety show" on a small ship permanently anchored in an inlet, a cold and dreary place with a casino, a topless bar, and pole dancing. We sat at a table, watching a topless young woman mechanically curl her body around a metal pole.

"This show is good," said Kulla, "but in Tallinn you get better quality."

Our host, smoking his Marlboros, gold signet ring glinting on his finger, replied that in Stockholm and Helsinki you got better shows still. The dancer looked cold and tired. She was related to someone, of course—everyone always was in this tiny country. We talked about her sister and her family. Katarina and I politely sipped our beer, and so did they. The evening wore on, more dancers arrived, and our hosts continued to discuss them in terms of their families and their dancing technique. One of the performers during the course of the evening, indeed, was pointed out as a well-known ballerina.

I still don't fully understand that evening. Did they secretly find it erotic? I can imagine few scenes less erotic than that cold bar, that polite conversation, those bland Marlboro Lights, and that relentless respectability. The "cultured' conversation about the sad dance, the cold and empty casino, the references to clubs in Tallinn, to Helsinki and Stockholm, may, I think, genuinely have been their idea of how people talked in the West, since those kinds of places were, of course, a Western import. But what did they imagine we would make of a place like that? Was that stiff and dull conversation a facade, a dull play for my and Katarina's benefit? Was it the case that because they knew that I was writing about them, they were on their best behaviour? And that I missed this because at home Toivo and Inna rarely tried to cover up family dysfunction? They seemed to me, in fact, always authentically themselves. That was their best trait.

Even so, without us, the pole dancing might have been slightly more raucous, or at least fun and transgressive. Perhaps with us there, a stiff and respectable conversation emerged in deference to respectability. But I don't think so. I think they genuinely didn't yet know the habits of the West and were trying to approximate something of our culture, without prejudice. The feminist debate about power and objectification, which no one in England, or Europe, or America, could possibly have missed, had not taken place in the Soviet Union. The notion that the dancers were being exploited seemed not to enter their minds. What they had grown up transgressing against was the repressive and stagnated system of actually existing socialism—and that was hardly a protest anymore. Perhaps the pole dancing, for them, was a gesture of protest against a system that no longer existed, and at the same time an uncritical appropriation of Western culture.

And what was it like for the young dancers? What happened to the dancer whose family was so well known to all at the table, or to the ballerina? What were their dreams, and where did they end up? Maybe it was a fleeting phase, and they look back now at what they did then with some private surprise, perhaps, at their audacity, or at how little they were paid, or at how much people drank and gambled. And they must think, I suppose, from time to time, about all the men, whatever went on after hours.

Many Estonian women at that time turned to prostitution. The *Baltic Observer* interviewed a prostitute who was a former medical student:

"If you ever fall in love and marry a poor man, won't you have problems sharing your life with him without payment?" the journalist asked.

"I wouldn't marry a poor man, regardless of how pleasant he is. I don't believe in love, since my society believes only in buying and selling. Money is the main thing in life."

Defiant collective capitalism; such was the zeitgeist. Post-Soviet seedy clubs were springing up everywhere. Pornography, suddenly, was spreading quickly—even in the cosy little post office in the village a single pornographic magazine made a brief appearance. The TV show that depicted Tallinn high life—Mafia life, perhaps—was full of prostitutes and strange clubs, crime, fast cars, and mobile phones. It became its own cliché; one expected nothing less (and nothing more) of the New Estonians.

In the spring a topless carwash opened in Tallinn. That was really strange, particularly given the Estonian climate. I theorised to Danny Miller, my supervisor:

The mockery of the transformation [worker to topless worker] effects a simultaneous humiliation of the abstract "worker" and the woman who works: it represents the world turned upside down in a carnivalesque joke intended to degrade the former system. This humiliation is a twin ideological sacrilege undermining both the "worker" and the "woman," the latter joining the "worker" as the second pillar of the Soviet state during Stalin's elevation of "mother-hood" to a quasi-sacred national duty. It is, then, a revenge on the Soviet system, but it is also, for both the women and the men, the workers and the employers, the promotion of identities which become deliberate symbols for what the system has turned into. In other words, one of the symbolic meanings of the act is the engagement of the self in a process of humiliation which expresses the commonly perceived moral degradation both of the Soviet state, and of the post-Soviet state. If the former was seen as primarily hypocritical in terms of how it dealt with sexuality and gender relations, the latter is seen as abandoning all moral intent, creating societies where money is the bottom line.

Danny didn't think much of that, quite rightly: "I am not sure about your topless interpretation which might have gone 'over the top' if you forgive the pun, but it is interesting." He didn't say so, but I think the point is that this kind of analysis is not fieldwork based, and therefore ignores both "culture," and individuals and their decisions.

There must have been a conversation, a moment when someone said, "Hey, that's a great idea!" Or, "Yeah, saw that in Riga!" Or, "Let's try it—it won't cost much." And there, paid a bit more than they might be as waitresses, or tipped a bit more, topless young women washed cars in the cold spring. I imagine the chemical cleansing agent in steaming water turning their fingers red and sore. I imagine dancing little steps and postures over the windscreens, Mafia types with short blond hair, on their mobiles, staring.

We think we know what they are like, those girls and those Mafia types, but we don't. All we know are clichés. Fieldwork can get you beyond the clichés, but only if you stay with the people for so long that you almost want to just stay forever. Then you have to leave, before you tip over the edge and go native. Imagining those cold hands, those postures, those customers, is not good enough, and even seeing them and talking to them is not good enough: that's just journalism. In anthropology, only participant observation—living and working side by side with people for a year or more, noting, observing, and thinking about their culture—gives you the authority to write about them. Or so we believed.

Ivar, the history teacher on the collective farm, would have despised the nihilism of the pole dancing and pornography: no cultural relativist, he. He was young and energetic, with a wispy, frankly unsuccessful beard. He was idealistic and perennially ironic, an expert on the history of the Swedes, and one of the main forces behind the adult school and the attempt to reestablish Swedishness in the area. His interest in this was abstract and historical—he himself was not a local and was without Swedish connections, though he did speak Swedish well.

Ivar had decided to stand to become a member of the local council. I went with him to put up notices of his political programme in the old barns where people collected their post. We cycled around the peninsula for hours, hanging flyers next to the tin post boxes with handwritten names on them. I remember the sense of purpose I felt whilst cycling on those long dirt roads, pine trees swaying. I have no idea now what his programme was, and I have a feeling that perhaps I never did know, but that didn't seem to matter much. I believed in his integrity and in his historical quest. We stopped at two Swedish farms to persuade people to come to his lecture about the Estonian Swedish history, which was scheduled for the next day. Two women did promise to come, I suspect to get us to go away, and then didn't. In fact only Katarina, two students, and I turned up. Ivar was very angry, and gave the whole lecture in a fast Swedish monotone, which the others could barely have understood, instead of in Estonian, as planned.

* * *

Ruth, my religious informant, took me to visit another Swedish farm. Leida and Lydia were two elderly cousins living in a flaking yellow farmhouse. Leida, in a poor apron and with longish grey-brown hair, greeted us at the door. Lydia had contracted polio as a child, and was paralysed as a result. Heavy and blond, she sat on a little square stool, which she used to heave herself about in the living room, where she also slept.

Ruth told her stock stories of survival and Christian miracles with a queasy kind of authority, and they both listened respectfully. Leida, after asking me if I was in a hurry in her peculiar, monotonous Swedish accent, said she would make coffee, and disappeared to the kitchen. She didn't say, but she was actually making lunch on the wood-fired stove: semolina porridge with apple sauce, cabbage, eggs, tiny fried sprats melting into a grey substance, biscuits, bread, and weak coffee. She brought it all to the table, and invited us to eat. Lydia remained on her low stool. There was a thick skin on the white porridge, and I stirred it, wondering if I could make myself eat it. Ruth sat next to me, happy in the warm kitchen with all the rich food. She dumped a hard-fried egg into my porridge and smiled benignly; I steeled myself and ate.

Leida had been to Sweden before, visiting relatives, and described how in Sweden there were no wood-fired stoves, only electrical ones. She talked about how rich Sweden was, how warm, how clean, how good the food was and how abundant. The others nodded. "Imagine that," they said calmly, and "Oh really," even though they must have heard it many times before, and imagined it, too. Their own kitchen was stocked with Swedish baking powder, vanilla sugar, cinnamon, and some coffee—otherwise there wasn't a lot, apart from several jars of poor-quality "Indian instant coffee" of uncertain origin.

Leida and Lydia had a different relationship to Sweden than the *kolkhozniks* in the blocks of flats; they were Swedish themselves, and they were old. They didn't discreetly interview me to find out what tea, what cereal, what brand of coffee, what kind of brandy or gin was "normal" and good, and which was not. They were not engaged in the process of becoming "normal" Estonians, unlike so many of the people in the village. After lunch they showed me a photo of a group of Swedish relatives standing outside a modern farmhouse, smiling at the camera, healthy and well. They had been picking potatoes. I wondered then if Leida and Lydia realised that potato picking by hand is only really a hobby in Sweden. The photograph might be interpreted differently in a culture where people still picked potatoes by hand as a matter of course in the small plots outside their houses.

Later that day Toivo and I drove to Österby, to the farm where he was doing some work. A thin old Alsatian was sitting in the garden, surrounded by many cats. We went through the farm entrance to the traditional cold room. There, on the floor, was a blood-specked pig's head in a tin bowl, blue eyes half closed. I jumped, then looked again—the pale lashes were so human. Toivo's salary this time was fresh meat, probably from that same pig. The farm woman asked Toivo a number of questions about me, in my presence, ranging from where I slept to how much I paid them in rent. Toivo said 300 kroon (£15) instead of the 400 kroon I actually paid, seemingly unaware that I was listening, and could understand what they said.

They left the room, and I sat waiting with a daughter and grandchild. The daughter was doing a crossword and the child was doodling. Everything was very quiet. The child put the pen in his mouth and spat it out, again and again, watching me. I clapped, quietly, to amuse him. His mother wouldn't speak. When Toivo finally came out, he ordered me to "Come on, please" in English. The farm woman laughed. She came out with some sprat in her hand, giving one to the old dog, and one each to the three cats. Toivo asked if I wanted to drive to the sea, and we did. The sun was a blood-red ball over the horizon, and everything else was icy white. The ice was thick enough to walk on by then, and soon it would be thick enough to drive on.

Not long after this, I got sick. The room, my room, felt drained of colour, and I felt sick of the place as well as in body, angry and frustrated. I wanted, suddenly, normal life and intelligent conversation. I felt the idiocy of talking in a language I knew only the barest bones of, the idiocy of never understanding properly, or saying what I deeply meant or thought. This was either the low point of my fieldwork, or a brief return to sanity from the practise of anthropological fieldwork. Or perhaps it was both.

When in despair, I always visited Veevi, and as soon as I recovered I did so again. She was very pleased that day because she had rung up a daily radio talk show about the new Estonia and its problems, and she had been on air.

"We scold each other," she said to me. "We eat each other up"—she pinched her throat and showed her teeth—"because we were occupied. If England had been occupied, it would have been the same."

"So, what did you say?" I asked.

She told me, at some length: that radio should broadcast moral debates and lectures on professional ethics; that the radio hosts must try to explain to the younger generation that the first ten years of building the first republic had also been hard; and that money must be found for concerts, exhibitions, and theatre. "Without culture," she said sternly, "there is nothing."

I can see her now, drilling me in exercises, standing in front of me, small and stout, waving her arms energetically, shouting, "*Üks, kaks, kolm* . . . one, two, three." She diagnosed my headache as all nerves (she was right about that), or possibly caused by an insufficient blood supply to the brain. She tried to teach me to breathe properly, and applied a Chinese salve to my toes to "purify" my blood. She complained, constantly, about the state of the nation.

"Sometimes I think the Estonians are worse than the Greeks," she said.

I smiled uncertainly.

"Oh yes," she said firmly, "they are worse than Jews, worse than Armenians. You can't trust them anymore. You must always control your money!"

After the war she had sold her diamond earrings for a pair of winter boots, and now she was afraid of selling her house for too little money. Controlling your money, counting your change, giving up on the idea that the Estonians were intrinsically more honest than the Russians, the Greeks, the Jews, and the Armenians was a concession for her, after a lifetime of patriotism and prejudice.

After that particular visit I came back to Pürksi quite tired. The wind was howling outside, and the village dogs seemed restless, barking more than usual. I slept in the afternoon, and then something seemed to be happening—there were people coming and going, talking in loud, worried voices. Inna went out, then came back, and telephoned. As usual they didn't tell me what was happening. When I went to see what was going on, Toivo, bare-chested, greeted me, and Inna, smiling, asked me if I was ill.

About this time Leigh decided that she couldn't face another lonely winter in Pürksi. She suddenly decided to leave, at once, before the deep winter set in. Alar, the English teacher, invited Katarina, Virve, and me to a small party to say goodbye to her. We drank tea and coffee, ate cakes, and drank strawberry *naps* (schnapps) and Estonian blue gin. We talked about the school and the village. Virve, enlivened by the *naps*, claimed that Laine surrounded herself with favourites, like Kulla, who got various privileges and who were not trained teachers. "We call her the postmistress," she said acidly, "because she used to work for the post."

Alar and his wife, Heli, more energetic than most of the people on the collective farm, talked about a measuring device for electricity, which one could buy and install, with some difficulty (both technical and bureaucratic), that would take the cheaper night rates into account. Alar was measuring the temperature of his hot water every day—never warmer than 30 degrees—in order to back up his protest at paying for hot water and not getting it. This was the first time I met them. They were to become my neighbours and friends, though I didn't know that then.

At home, Toivo was drunk and sad because a friend of his had died. He had died because some work at the *kolkhoz* had been given to a younger man. Timo later said he'd heard that he had drank himself to death. Someone else said he had died of a heart attack, or perhaps blood poisoning. Without a functioning state, causes of death were uncertain. He didn't reach the life expectancy of the times, that dismal 60.5 years for men. Perhaps he actually did die of the combination of the causes people talked about, all of which were implicated in that low life expectancy; perhaps he died from alcohol, and a heart attack, and blood poisoning, and losing his job, and giving up. Toivo invited me to the funeral, and then drank more and more, pacing the narrow corridor. Inna was gone. For the first time I fled him, and the flat, and went over to Katarina's to sleep on her sofa. She was knitting on her eternal red dress, and gave me Swedish chocolate and talked sagely about alcoholics she had known, before bedding me down with a blanket.

The next day I waited for Toivo at noon, like we had agreed, to go to the funeral. At 11:30 he had knocked at my door, and stood in the doorway swaying, trying hard to concentrate, still drunk from the night before, asking me to be ready soon. I went to the school to eat, and sat with Selma, the elderly school accountant, in worried silence. Then I went to Kulla, and told her what had happened. She looked at me with some concern, and said that she would come and speak to him. I felt an anthropological duty to attend a funeral (notes on cosmology, notes on death), and this seemed my best opportunity. I asked, therefore, Kulla to come. She refused, of course. I waited for a while, and then went back to the flat to find Inna on the phone. Toivo had already gone. My chapter on death didn't happen.

Later Inna, for the first time, made spaghetti in a lumpy, salty white sauce. Toivo was out, and all was quiet. Somebody—presumably Toivo—came back very late, then there was a crash, and then silence. The next day Inna cooked an unexpectedly good dinner: tiny pieces of mutton with cabbage, carrots, and potatoes. Toivo was flushed and bloated and quiet. Inna left soon after dinner. I went to my room with a cup of tea, and Toivo came in with an unprecedented plate of stuffed cookies, filled with condensed milk, and apples, saying, "It's no good this drinking tea with nothing to eat." He was making amends. His kindness had the effect of suddenly making the whole situation real. It struck me then with some force that I was not always going to live like this, and, also, that important parts of this experience were already over and done with.

Now I think about the children. Ene, the girl, was translucent, and quiet. Erki was in my English class, a tough kid, but sweet, too. He tittered knowingly with the other kids, and seemed quite happy. I wonder about the effect on Ene and Erki of Toivo's drinking. Inna was usually smiling and quiet. Toivo, even when he was sober, vacillated between suspicion, heartiness, and a depressed silence. They had no family life to speak of. The children came and went, and so did the parents. What did they make of me, I also wonder now, with all my books, my polite and broken Estonian, my obvious or unexpected questions, and nebulous topic of research? I have no idea, but I suppose I must have been discussed, though it never seemed so at the time. So little was discussed in my presence, but perhaps in my absence a completely different life was going on. They might, at least, have been speculating or gossiping about me—at the time it never occurred to me that they did, but now I think they certainly must have.

There were two modes to my experience of being in Estonia, one almost surreal and extraordinary, and the other very real—reassuringly real—which had something to do with being in that landscape, so grey, so ordinary, so reassuring. November was cold, though: minus 16 degrees during the day and minus 20 at night for days. A kind of weather chauvinism set in, with people saying that minus 15 is nothing out of the ordinary—wait until the temperature drops to minus 25 or so . . . One cold afternoon in November I went for a walk to see the red sun setting in the white sky over the icy fields, the snow like fine arctic dust.

Of course the November cold snap didn't last. The temperature came back to around zero, and our plans to drive over the ice to Haapsalu, which had come to nothing anyway because of Toivo's drinking spree, were shelved, as was my aesthetic exhilaration. The reality of the collective farm hit me again—the constant cabbage and potatoes, the dirt, the drinking, and, again, the fact of living in an environment where I could express and understand only slightly more than the barest minimum.

My imagination, though, didn't seem to properly encompass the notion that what I didn't understand might be significant, and that I was therefore perhaps not just missing individual words but also essential meaning. The limited communication I had with people was so perfectly matched by the aesthetic of the village; the limits of meaning reflected in the limits of the architecture, the crumbling concrete and broken glass, the permanent deep pool of frothy water on the other side of our living block caused by a broken pipe. It was an aesthetic of disconnections and disjointed meaning, of loss of memory and narrative, reflected in my mind by the disconnections in my Estonian.

The small improvements in my language seemed, deceptively, to be reflected in the small improvements, or changes, in the village, bridging the gap of strangeness. Thus the day in September when they finally took down the *kolkhoz* sign and replaced it with a sign for the small bank office that was going to open in the culture hall was followed shortly afterwards by the first day I felt that I was really taking part in a conversation, and understanding what people were saying. My progress in the language seemed to reflect the progress of the place. The bank office never did open. The sign, however, remained for a while; another lost future. There was a kind of madness in those connections, I now think, a slightly hallucinatory quality, and no wonder: how strange it all was.

Haapsalu in November was empty of cars, and seemingly almost of people. Women pulled children on sledges, and there were frost patterns like stars on the windows of the low wooden houses. One night I visited the new restaurant, Rootsi Kohvik (Swedish Café), with Katarina. A fragile crescent moon hung above the surreal miniature high-rise outside, almost square in shape, built as a training ground for firefighters. Afterwards we went to the cinema and saw *Accidental Hero*, starring Dustin Hoffman. The auditorium was cold, with wooden seats, and the sound of the projector was very loud. The film, with Russian and Estonian subtitles, was not dubbed. There were about twelve people there, more than I had ever seen before.

A few days later we had lunch in the main restaurant in Haapsalu, a Soviet-style self-service canteen. It was a huge room, with few tables, at which two separate groups of men were seated. In the ice-cold lobby a Russian woman guarded the lavatories, selling rough pieces of lavatory paper. Two younger Russian women, heavily made up, were waiting, possibly for customers. An old man sat on a bench opposite, smoking. The food—a few plates of dried-out potato salad, a choice between *kotlet* and schnitzel, with potatoes and cabbage—was dismal. I asked for the schnitzel, and the pale, silent woman fished out a small piece of charred, dried fat. I had the cutlet instead, a black and hard piece of meat, and found pieces of what I hoped was bone and dreaded was teeth in it. The cabbage was too sour to eat. The men stared at us in silence.

We went to the café next door, and had some coffee poured from a 1960s-looking urn with a handle, and a dry piece of cake.

Unlike the restaurant, there were some Western signs there—adverts for Wrigley's chewing gum, Finnish chocolates, Fanta, and Coca-Cola, though no actual chewing gum or chocolates or soft drinks. It was very easy to imagine what it must have been like a year or two earlier, though, with the same empty shelves, the same weak coffee in glasses with sugar already measured up.

Afterwards we wandered through the run-down Russian Orthodox cemetery. There were Estonian, Russian, German, and Swedish names on the headstones. At the end was a chapel. A woman in a headscarf was on her knees cleaning the floor with a dirty rag. She called the priest out to meet us. He was Estonian, young and thin and bearded. He greeted us eagerly, and showed us the icons and the books, and sang for us in Old Church Slavonic, the Orthodox liturgical language. He told us about the controversy now in the Estonian Orthodox community about whether they should stay under Moscow, or go over to Constantinople. Before we left, he blessed us.

I came back to the flat to find Toivo on his own, hanging around the cupboard in the kitchen where I suspected he kept a supply of vodka. Glassy-eyed and unsteady, he told me I should have driven over the ice.

"But there is water on top of the ice," I said. "It was there yesterday. It's breaking up."

"Sa kardad [You are afraid]," he said, swaying, and laughed at me.

I took refuge in my room, feeling that I was beginning to understand the urge for high culture in the Soviet empire—I craved poetry and classical music, some pathos to make sense of the poverty and dirt and idiotic drunkenness. The people on the collective farm had little connection either with the land or with high culture. They just got by, day by day, enduring the uncertainty, the confusion, and the quiet fear: fear of unemployment, fear of Russia, fear of the future. Many people were leaving, too. You would see an old lorry parked outside a window and a group of men slowly transferring the belongings of a family through the window onto the lorry. They stood there, smoking and chatting quietly, languidly moving the few things they had to move. Then they'd be gone, and that was that.

November merged into December. I visited as many people as I could out on the farms. Many of the people there were born on the peninsula, and some had grown up in the farmhouses where they still lived. I had a new farm acquaintance called Terje. She was from town originally, bored and languid, unused to the country and the hard work. She had two young girls and a foster daughter. I liked being on that farm and, particularly, visiting her animals, her pigs and cows, and her calves, licking my hand with their coarse, wet tongues.

I often came back to Leida and Lydia, too, mostly because I liked them. I felt at home with their Swedishness; they felt familiar to me. They were, also, welcoming and generous, giving me lunch or cake every time I visited. Lunch might be potatoes boiled in their skins, with some fried herring, homogenised at the bottom of an old tin bowl. It was easy, when we talked, to forget this quiet poverty: the milk in a tin jug, the tin bowl for the scraps of herring, and the bucket of water from the well. They never complained.

After one visit I said I was thinking of driving to the sea, and invited them to come. Lydia suggested that Leida come with me. We then decided instead to go to Pürksi, where Lydia had a sister. They both got changed, and Lydia, laboriously getting around on her little stool, went to the cupboard to find a gift for me, a stale Swedish mini Mars bar sent by some relative long ago, which she threw over to me in return for the lift. We got her into the car with not too much trouble. I had assumed, once there, that we would be invited into her sister's house. I think Lydia and Leida thought so, too, because they brought the stool. But there was a tractor in the way, and the sister's husband showed no inclination to move it. Nor did he come up to the car to greet us. After some time, the sister came out and sat with us in the car for a while, a pale grandchild with a dirty face on her lap. She said we had to sit there, since Lydia couldn't get out.

Eventually we left. There was, by then, a dreadful stench in the car. We drove by the sea, which was frozen and beautiful, and Leida and I got out for a bit. At the house Lydia refused further help, and said she wanted to be out in the fresh air for a while. She sat on the ice-cold stone steps and waited for me to be gone.

I also met a Swedish farmer called Astrid, the retired secretary of the village council. She invited me for milking and dinner, having heard me say that I had never milked a cow. She met me on the step with outstretched arms, and then we went in. I waited for a long time in the living room, basking in the warmth of the old stove behind me, attempting a little conversation with her son's girlfriend from Tallinn, but without much success. The son was silent, tinkering with something at a desk, and Astrid was, I think, feeding her husband in the kitchen. He was Estonian, a returned deportee, silent and distant, marked by his experiences.

Astrid made me dress in special milking clothes: an old cardigan and a pair of trousers, a hat and scarf, an old coat and special boots. We got the sterilised milk cans, and went out to the barn, where two black and glossy cows stood happily chewing the cud, alongside six hens and a white rooster from Krasnodar, perched on a beam. Astrid washed the teats with water, and spread a little Vaseline on them to stop them from cracking. She showed me how to sit on the low stool, close to the warm cow, and press and pull the teats at the same time, the lovely intimate practise of milking. As we were milking peacefully side by side, we had an interesting conversation about cows, and about the *kolkhoz*, which continued inside.

Then we had dinner: pork with onion gravy, homemade sauerkraut and boiled potatoes, followed by whipped cream and homemade cranberry compote. It's hard to describe how delicious that dinner was in the context of the food I ate every day. During the war, if you were living with rationing, you might have fantasised about a dinner like that. I saved Astrid's recipe for the sauerkraut, but never tried it. I suspect it wouldn't have worked as well outside the specific bacterial environment of the farm—that particular probiotic brew creating the sourness of sauerkraut. They were virtually self-sufficient on that farm. They had milk, eggs, chicken, pork, beef, potatoes, peas, onions, apples, carrots, cabbage, cucumbers, and cranberries, and mushrooms in the forest and fish from the sea. But perhaps that incredible meal was unusual for them, too—in fact, in retrospect I think it must have been a feast, presented in the typical low-key Estonian way.

Astrid's family had lived on this farm for generations. The old farmhouse burnt down in 1974, and they rebuilt it more or less as it was. It had the same rooms and facilities the old farmhouse had: wood-burning stoves for heating and cooking, cold larders for meat and milk. No refrigeration. No running water and no sanitation. But even without those things, the home and the dinner felt so luxurious. There was something here, still, of the culture of the independence era, despite the fire, the deportation, and the collectivisation. That culture of farming self-sufficiency hadn't survived in the village, but it survived here, I think because Astrid was so competent and so strong.

As I ate, Astrid talked. She was angry both with the collectivisation and with the demise of the *kolkhoz*. She talked about the war, and how the Germans evacuated Estonians from the Russian border, and moved them to Noarootsi, where there were many abandoned farms after the Swedes left. The refugees, she said, had already suffered years of disorder in the Soviet Union. They didn't know how to take care of things, and didn't care. They burnt furniture and beams to keep warm.

"The abandoned cattle," she continued, "were screaming in their pastures."

I looked up from my plate. She had actually said that. It seemed that she said it not because she could no longer remember the Swedish word for the sound cows make when they are distressed, but because she thought "screaming" was the better word. She felt their suffering.

After dinner I drove on towards Österby, and then out to the sea. There were some strong lights on in Haapsalu, and the sea was only partly icy. Pürksi, later, seemed more alien than usual, with its dilapidated blocks of flats, and its rubbish bags torn to pieces and spread around by the dogs. The snow had turned to slush, revealing the dirt. In the flat, Toivo was unexpectedly grinding meat, alone, in the kitchen. There was, also, an unprecedented jug of mint tea on the table, somewhat making up for the bleak reality of Pürksi.

That same evening my friend Josh rang up from New York. The telephones worked only intermittently, and international calls barely worked at all. This call, oddly, was clear and uninterrupted, and Josh launched into a monologue of the amazing people he had just met, the not-for-profit entrepreneurs, the human rights activists, the local food proponents.

"I've just milked a cow in a nineteenth-century shed," I said finally, "and here you are, ringing me up from New York."

"From Manhattan, even," he said, and laughed.

I suddenly longed to be in Manhattan, too. This poor and remote village was becoming too real to me, maybe partly because it reminded me in so many ways of Sweden. I felt I knew it all so well, that landscape, those people. I was beginning to take the bad food, the silences, and the cold for granted. It was the new normal.

EIGHT

Winter

In December I finally made the decision to move. I went for an early morning walk in the icy wind. Everything was grey and silver: ice, concrete, sky, except an orange old sign in Russian on the ground, thrown away and partially snowed over. I felt increasingly wary of Toivo, who was now working regularly, and looked at me quietly and defiantly. He got paid in food, and borrowed my car to get around, though he didn't quite want to ask. One day he offered, insistently, to wash it, which I said wasn't necessary, until I understood what he wanted. He returned that day carrying his wages: a few sacks of potatoes. After lunch I went for a walk, past some men working in the forest, dark faces, white-blond hair, beards and moustaches. The snow was heavy, and I saw elk prints. I ate a handful of snow, a remembered childhood taste.

I crossed the square that night to tell Katarina about my decision to leave. The night was archaically beautiful, three elements coming together in harmony: ice, silence, and huge stars in a black heaven. It was winter.

I set my students to write essays about Christmas:

On Christmas time we have a fir-tree in our house and it is decorated with many decorations. While we were eating, somebody knocked at our door. It was Santa Claus. (Actually it was our neighbour) So, he came in and sat by the Christmas tree. And he had a quite big sack with him and there were the Christmas presents of course! That we could get our presents, we had to sing, dance or do something funny. I sang a Christmas song, my father danced and my mother kissed Santa Claus, And then we got our presents.

x-mas

x-mas in Estonia is new thing. Because few years ago, when we were in Soviet Union we had no x-mas. Then was another party, which was almost the same, only it was later. But now it is like everywhere, I think. People are at home with their parents etc. Of course we have special Christmasfood. One old tradition is that in Christmas night, must be food at the table, because then . . . I don't know what then will be. But I'm not very interested about it (all Christmas I mean), because I don't believe it all (Jesus Christ etc) But if it's true, then after death I'm going to hell. Sad but true.

All the subtle signs of globalisation spoke to me. One day there was a Michael Jackson sticker on the vase of Christmas decorations on the kitchen table. Ene was a fan. I told her he had been arrested, and was surprised by the fact that she already knew, and knew enough to say that she thought the sister, Latoya, who I think had testified against him in the case, was crazy. I had never thought much about Michael Jackson and his trials and tribulations, but nevertheless at that moment I felt so comforted by this sign that the village, the peninsula, and Estonia were moving towards the globalised culture I was part of. There was another little sticker next to Michael Jackson, a little oval I recognised as originating from an orange saying DOLE COSTA RICA. It was a faint reminder of another life—a life of oranges; and fridges filled with yogurt, cheeses, vegetables and fruit, prepacked chicken, and sushi; and newspapers and books and magazines on kitchen tables. DOLE COSTA RICA—this little oval flag from a single orange, probably a gift, had made its unchartered way into this particular kitchen in this particular village, saved by a thirteen-year-old girl who collected references from the West, as they all did. I looked at it and my mouth watered.

Before Christmas, Inna, the school secretary, offered me her flat, perhaps encouraged to do so by Laine, the headmistress, who probably thought of my stay with Inna and Toivo as a potential problem. I had already warned them that I might leave, but now I had to tell them that I really was going. We sat in the kitchen. They visibly stiffened, and didn't say very much. Inna disappeared out somewhere.

There was a storm, and there was no water, electricity, or heating. Children, tucked into old Swedish ski jackets, were gliding around on water-covered ice patches outside the flat, screaming and struggling against the wind. Toivo, who had been sober for a while, looked subdued. Nothing more was said about it.

Virve, the teacher from Finland, had her mother over for a visit. That same evening she played the piano for Virve's dance class. There was only one student there, Helen, a pale and ambitious twelfth grader. She and Virve, and Katarina and I, learnt to dance a square tango, and a slow and complex Polish folk dance in four stages. The music, that simple piano played by the old lady with snow-white hair, was so beautiful in the cold hall, candles ready in case of another power cut.

I stayed on for a little while after the flat had been offered. Toivo was restless and irritable, moving between the kitchen and the living room like a caged animal. He compulsively watched American films on Moscow TV, dubbed into Russian. One time he angrily demanded that I put a button back on his shirt. The next day I saw a porn magazine by the television. The children kept out of his way. Inna, on the other hand, was cooking up a storm. One day for the first time we got chicken for lunch, a large chicken, dry and chewy, probably an old hen. That same evening we had cabbage pirogis for dinner. Toivo ate, sighing loudly and somewhat theatrically; Inna sat staring out the window, silent and impervious; Ene came gliding in, and quickly ate a bun and drank a glass of milk, standing by the kitchen sink.

Earlier that day I had looked for an abandoned house I had found recently to photograph it, but I couldn't find it again, and instead rambled on almost to the sea. I found an abandoned shed, and went inside. The hide of some animal was spread out on the ground, with wet tufts of hair, and there was a faint smell of meat and blood. It looked as though a sacrifice had taken place. I left quickly, and got a lift back with a man; we didn't say much.

I went to see Katarina afterwards, and found her with some fish, three perch. She had found, to her horror, that they were still alive after she bought them, tossing noisily in the kitchen in a flimsy plastic bag. After asking me to kill them first, she did it herself, like the sea captain's daughter she was, and cooked them, too. It was the first fish I had had on the collective farm—no one fished much anymore. We ate, and watched a strange pop programme on her TV. The lead guitarist had pink-red hair, and three girls danced on top of a car, eating bananas. Katarina frowned. She didn't like the subsequent act in the programme either: a collection of suited men wearing Palestinian shawls.

"It's not right to joke about serious matters," she said disapprovingly, as she knit her red dress. It had become twisted, a long red tube, and she looked at it helplessly, but kept on knitting nevertheless.

That week we were told that there would be no more hot water until February because a pipe had burst and they were "renovating" the system. Up until then there had only been a little tepid water once a week. One evening we did suddenly have hot water, and took turns showering in the dirty but at least now quite warm little bathroom. I walked out later, into the black and starry early evening, and saw flames in the workshop, and shadows of men against the windows. I came closer, and saw the men shovelling coal into the old furnace, blackened faces and hands, orange flames and huge furnace. It was like a socialist realist painting. It seems there was coal again. The next day Inna enquired, and was told that there would be hot water every evening from then on. It lasted a day. The next evening, there was only about half an hour's worth of tepid water, and then even that came to an end.

Katarina and I celebrated my new flat with dinner at the Rootsi Kohvik in Happsalu. The atmosphere was a little strained between a Russian group of guests and the few Estonians in the room. The silent and correct Estonian waiter brought the food quickly. Afterwards we went again to the cinema—cold, uncomfortable, and next to empty. Two girls giggled helplessly in front of us as the story—*The Prince of Tides*—unfolded.

Soon I moved into the new flat. It had a small hall with a narrow shelf on which stood an old and semifunctioning telephone and assorted knick-knacks. The kitchen and balcony were to the right, with a dirty old stove with four buckled plates, two of which worked. There was a large fridge with Swedish magnets stuck to the door, a cold store full of old glass jars, a rickety table with two chairs, a sink and some cupboards. There were rotten carrots, sour milk, some frozen pieces of fat, and four dirty eggs in the fridge.

The room was on the other side of the hall, with a bed, a sofa, the ubiquitous wall unit, a big old Russian TV, and a curiously English-looking broken electric fire with a fake log and brick effect. The bathroom was small and blue, with some silver-grey foam squares on the floor. The bath, also, was painted blue, as was, strangely, the inside of the lavatory. Again, I cleaned obsessively, though I tried to keep the eggs. They turned out to be rotten.

This block of flats—three stories instead of two—dated from the 1970s, and had a flushing lavatory. There was no hot water, of course, but I could keep clean, as I had done all along, by heating water on the stove, pouring it into a bucket, and sponging myself down. I relished being in the flat. It was as if I was acting out an immigrant's story of coming first to a cheap hotel, then to lodgings, and finally to my own place. It wasn't just the relief to be away from Toivo, though there was that, of course. It was also the fact that I was progressing in that small world, following a narrative of progress and assimilation that was hard to resist.

The flat was across the hall from Alar and Heli, the English teacher and his wife, who soon became friends. They took me shopping in Haapsalu. We drove through a snowstorm over the ice, skidding over the vast expanse in the near whiteout with a giddy sense of the five meters of water beneath us, and the frightening possibility of missing the intermittent flimsy snow poles on the ice that formed the path over the sea. We made it across, and went to the new little supermarket, where they bought the last box of corn flakes and an ice cream each, to eat in the snowstorm.

Now that I was living on my own I was buying my own food, and became more aware of prices. The cost of that box of corn flakes was about five hours of lessons, in other words about a day's work for Alar. Before the currency reform in 1992, when the Estonian kroon was introduced as the only legal tender in Estonia, the economy was divided into an eastern and a western zone. The value of the rouble had been set at 10 percent of the kroon. People with savings saw the worth of what they had in the bank decimated: 1,000 roubles, a decent saving, approximately equivalent to £1,000 or so before 1989 (though you couldn't, of course, exchange it), became 100 kroons in the bank, worth no more than £10. It was the price paid for independence. The rouble itself was going down faster than the kroon, so hard as it was, it was a good decision. In September 1993 the average monthly wage in Estonia was 800 kroon (about £40). It was, of course, an anomalous economic situation. By 2005 the average monthly wage was about 8,000 kroon, increasing, by

2008, to nearly 13,000 kroon—Estonia did well, and was about to do better. But they didn't know that then.

In 1993 the Soviet hard-currency stores had multiplied, and still carried almost only Western goods, whilst the old shops sold mainly produce from the Eastern Bloc. There were also some new Western-style supermarkets. Even though the difference between the two kinds of shops was slowly eroding, the price differential between formerly Soviet and Western goods was still huge. Food—wine, coffee, cereal, and biscuits—imported from the West sold for Western prices. Food imported from eastern Europe sold for eastern European prices.

Western products, despite the fact that they were enormously expensive, were seen as superior ("normal"), whilst products made in countries of the former Soviet Union were often suspected of being polluted by chemicals or Chernobyl radiation. The private shop in the village, for example, started stocking Ariel washing powder, at a cost of about 35 kroons (£1.75), six times more than the local powder, which itself had increased so much in price that it represented nearly an hour's average work. The high cost, however, did not mean that Ariel was treated like an exclusive boutique washing powder. People knew that it was "normal," and its superiority was defined in strictly functional terms. Given that the Estonian washing powder turned clothes of any light colour grey, that was perhaps not surprising. I used it, for my own complicated existential reasons, washing clothes in my bucket hanging them to dry in my bathroom.

People who had been abroad, usually to Helsinki, kept stockpiles at home of flour, pasta, rice, and soap—all things formerly unavailable. Now you could buy them at a lower price in Estonia than in Finland. The 1989–93 period was a difficult time, culminating in the Russian constitutional crisis. People didn't know which way things would go. It was only two years earlier that they had had rationing and food queues.

The school cook, large and alcoholic, swaying as she dished out the food, experimented with a private enterprise one day. School meals were already privatised—you paid for your meals before entering the dining room, and got a ticket saying exactly what you had paid for: so many pieces of bread, the main meal (mainly boiled potatoes, picked by the students from the school fields), pudding and tea, if available. That particular day she had made some portions of pancakes with jam, and sold them for 2 kroons (10 pence) herself. That was about the price of a full meal; this was an impromptu privatisation within the privatisation. It seemed like a new beginning, but to my knowledge it was never repeated. Even though the pancakes sold out, her enterprise went by the wayside, like the branch of the bank that never opened.

Estonia was a society in transformation. Things that had been normal a year or two ago were now more and more seen as "not normal." Amitav Ghosh, in his wonderful book about a remote Egyptian village, *In an Antique Land*, describes the fellaheens' relationship to the concept of "development":

> I had an inkling then of the real and desperate seriousness of their engagement with modernism, because I realized that the fellaheen saw the material circumstances of their lives in exactly the same way that a university economist would: as a situation that was shamefully anachronistic, a warp upon time; I understood that their relationships with the objects of their everyday lives was never innocent of the knowledge that there were other places, other countries which did not have mud-walled houses and cattle-drawn ploughs, so that those objects, those houses and ploughs, were insubstantial things, ghosts displaced in time, waiting to be exorcized and laid to rest.

My friends and informants would have understood that feeling. They knew that not only was the collective farm itself rendered obsolete by the changes in the country, but so was the greater part of their material culture: the dusty and dilapidated culture house, the agricultural machinery slowly rusting in a backyard, the crumbling concrete staircases, the broken Ladas, the Russian kettles and polyester clothes. They used to be the Westerners of the Soviet Bloc; now they were the Easterners of Europe.

People had been waiting for the new wood-chip heating unit to come from Sweden, the best part of the aid package from the twin town. The thing finally arrived, and was installed, I think, with some difficulty. The piping was too rusty for it to work properly, but it was a start. Two unemployed Swedes were sent over—this was, in fact, a Swedish-style job creation scheme—to do the snagging after the installation, because the Swedes didn't trust the Estonians with proper and thorough cleaning and painting. They were not a success, however, doing a cursory job, and spending their evenings in the bar complaining of boredom and isolation. There was still no hot water, and not much heating either.

January turned cold. The fields through my window were snow-covered, a comforting monochrome at early afternoon dusk, like the grey screen of my Mac laptop in front of me. Temperatures dipped to minus 33 degrees centigrade at night, and there was not much heating in the flats. Heli and Alar lent me a spare electric radiator. They had been sued for not paying their heating bills, which came to 500 kroons, about £25, per month. His salary then was about 800 kroons and she had only 150 in child support. There was little communal heating, despite the bills, and people had to rely on private radiators, and it was patently absurd that anyone in those circumstances would pay the bill. There were scenes in the teachers' room between Alar and Ivar, now an elected member of the council. Alar was the only person to protest.

When Leigh left she gave me her American therapy tape on depression to keep, which I listened to whilst I did the cleaning or washing up. It was a voice from another culture. Some rare days were blue and sunny. Children bundled up in donated Swedish ski clothes tottered about. Most days were not. The cold was intense, the kind of cold that makes breathing hard. The kind of cold that is actually frightening. One day, without thinking about it, I stepped out on my balcony with wet hair. It froze instantly. I thought if I were, by any chance, to be locked out on the balcony in this cold, without a coat, I would die.

About this time I visited Felix Sedman, an elderly Estonian Swede, to invite him to a showing of a Swedish TV documentary about the peninsula. Sedman had been interviewed in it, but no one had thought to invite him. He seemed not to remember the documentary at first, but eventually he did, and accepted my invitation in a hesitant deep voice. He was an artist, and his back garden was full of his sculptures. He told me to go to the back and take a look at his parents, and there they were, moulded in concrete and painted yellow, on a pedestal of grey Soviet bricks, inscribed MIN MOR O FAR. "My Mother and Father." A memorial. It struck me again, seeing that, how sad this area must have been after the war, with half the people gone, family and friends dead or abroad, and traumatised strangers from Russia taking over the farms.

The night of the documentary I was tired. My car had got stuck in deep snow miles from anywhere as the early afternoon dusk was falling. The back wheels spun uselessly, and I was at least an hour's walk from the nearest house, which in that severe cold was not a trivial matter. I had to get out of the car again and again to stuff branches under the tyres to give them traction. Eventually it worked.

Later I picked up Felix Sedman with his wife. The show began downstairs in the students' common room, a cold basement with some chairs and a table, on which stood a lamp, the shade of which was a bleak homemade creation of barbed wire and a raised scene with an old sofa and a few armchairs.

The Swedish documentary was saved from outright sentimentality only by the outspoken nature of the Estonian participants.

Felix Sedman said on camera that nothing would ever be as it was before the war because the younger generation was so lazy. Mayor Ülo Kalm, asked whether that was true, retorted that Sedman knew nothing about anything, since he was a pensioner and only moved between his house and the shop. They were both in the audience. Sedman and his wife sat in stony silence, refusing all offers of food or more comfortable chairs.

"That was nice, wasn't it?" said Katarina afterwards, oblivious to the atmosphere. She had saved the best sandwiches to take home, which she thought was only fair since she had made them. I refused to take anything, and went home, depressed, to read Freud's "Dora" case study.

Slowly I began to feel at home in my flat. Virve lived in the block opposite. I would see her open her curtains in the kitchen, notice me, and move back inside. Her Mazda was like a chubby little red bus in the snow behind a rusty, lean Lada. Katarina, also in the same block, was forever airing her rugs on the balcony, forever cleaning. She feared that Dumble, her mouse, had died, and had stopped leaving food for it, to the relief of Virve, who had disapproved of the mouse feeding from the beginning. That block also housed the dormitories for the high school borders, who trundled through the snow to the school.

One evening I lost my key, so I went to Alar and Heli's for help. They called Inna, the owner of the flat, gave me a drink, and then drove with me to her parents to pick up a spare key. We came back to their flat, and had several more drinks: apricot *naps*, first with orange juice and then with lemonade, enormously sweet, as they liked it. I had one of Alar's cigarettes to combat the enveloping sense of sweetness. They also offered me tea, showing me the range of different tea bags they had. I chose the Lipton Earl Grey, which led to a discussion—again—of the different teas available. Was Earl Grey, they asked, better than English Breakfast? What made some Earl Grey teas better than others, and was Lipton a good make? They had tried fifteen different kinds of tea from the *kaubahall* (supermarket)—you could buy them by the tea bag—but they hadn't yet discovered which was the best brand. They were trying to construct a hierarchy of taste out of the new confusion of Western products, and I was their arbiter of good taste, their informant about the West.

The *naps* was going to my head, and they brought out their photo albums. I looked with fascination—they looked completely different in each picture, with different styles of clothing, hairstyles, and settings, which gave them an exciting, almost gangsterish quality. In one photo they were visiting Finland, dressed in Estonian traditional dress. Next they were in tight jeans and sleeveless T-shirts, hair punkish and semi-shaved. Then Alar, alone, was in Canada, in front of a large selection of brandy in a liquor store; making faces at two male mannequins; standing by a lake with a group of relatives, Canadian Estonians. After that, both of them were on holiday in Sweden, a big dark man putting an arm around each of them with a serene and inebriated smile. Everything was changing. It was only the dire poverty on the collective farm that kept things reasonably static.

In mid-February it was still minus 20 degrees outside, and so cold inside the school the children sat huddled in their Swedish ski jackets and woolly hats. The teachers were tired and subdued, except, of course, for Ivar, who was always energetic. I talked to Timo. In the middle of our conversation he suddenly stopped and then said, "I'm calculating how many weeks I have left here." I knew what he meant—we were due to leave at about the same time. I walked through the grey wintry dusk, as I did most days, snow blowing across the road, a yellow star-frosted window in a farmhouse in the woods. Just when it felt as though winter would never end, it did. That day was the last day of proper winter. From one day to the next the sun set in a sky that was light blue, pink, and orange, and winter dusk turned into blue twilight. The snow on the roofs dripped all day in the sun, and huge, lethal icicles hung from every roof.

Leigh's replacement finally arrived. Her name was Sally, a librarian and writer from rural Canada. She was well read, ironic and self-deprecating, with nervous habits and large, anxious brown eyes. I took her to the cinema in Haapsalu—*My Girl*—and to dinner at the Rootsi Kohvik. She was a little disorientated, and had clearly come on a whim, to get away from someone or something. She had met a little boy that morning in the village who answered "hello" back to her greeting. She was cheered up by his knowledge of English until she heard him practising behind her, "Hello. Hello. Hello. Hello."

She talked already about people not smiling at her, or greeting her. This was tricky, I knew. Leaving my flat was always an exercise in small gestures: How far away must a person be for greetings to be unnecessary? From what distance can you perceive a nod? How to acknowledge people, and how to be acknowledged, was problematic for all the foreigners—for Leigh and Sally, the Estonian impassivity seemed hostile. I felt a mild sense of solidarity from our shared northern apartness but smiled too much, as did Katarina. Virve, being Finnish, did better. If there was a good reason to smile she did, otherwise not. Sally, more fragile than any of us, found that the lack of warmth wore her down.

Independence Day in Estonia is 24 February. At eleven o'clock people gathered in the stone-cold culture hall, all the schoolchildren and thirty-five or so adults, including the teachers. The school orchestra, the children's choir, the women's choir, and the students' dance team performed; three girls read poems, and we sung the complex and difficult national anthem. Proceedings were interrupted twice by Ruth, who made several generally unwelcome religious speeches. Her grandson, Samuel, who was conducting the orchestra, walked out at one point, looking tense and drawn. People applauded lamely after the first speech, but during the second one a small elderly man, usually drunk, though not, I think, on this occasion, tried to stop her, as did Samuel, and she slightly shortened her speech. The man, she told me later, was a "notorious communist." Magnus, one of my best students, was the standard bearer, and carried the flag up on the stage, grinning self-consciously. Ülo, the mayor, made a speech about the hard work of independence, and Laine, the headmistress, spoke, unexpectedly thanking Virve, Katarina, and me. We had to go up to the stage to receive Estonian plastic flags and be applauded. Virve and I struggled out of our coats for the sake of decorum, whilst Katarina calmly strolled up in her hideous pink ski jacket and red Helly Hansen mittens.

Later there was Spumante, coffee, cakes, and chocolates in the school. Laine, a manifestly insincere expression on her face, told me that I had now seen how they feel that Estonia is its own country. Virve, listening in, looked inscrutable. She didn't think much of Laine's patriotism, and told me later that the year before Ivar had been organising it, and at the last minute went on a trip to Viljandi with some other people instead of attending his own event. The celebration would have come to nothing if Selma, the school accountant, hadn't stepped in and made a speech about her childhood in pre-war independent Estonia, and about the Soviet times, and how things were now. We drank the Spumante and the coffee, and ate the cakes, and life went on. My plastic Estonian flag stood on my kitchen table for a while, then disappeared.

In March the school organised an excursion for the teachers to a swimming pool outside Haapsalu. They must have run out of chlorine for the pool; the cloudy water smelled indefinably musty. It had an even dirtier foot bath, which everyone nimbly sidestepped. The atmosphere was exuberant, though. Vladimir Belovas, Laine's husband, was there, in tight swimming trunks. He and Alar, in equally tight trunks, played a ball game in the pool, diving like sleek dolphins. I found Vladimir later alone in the sauna, a big man with an indifferent gaze. He had been the director of the collective farm, and now he was running a garage in Haapsalu. I introduced myself.

"I know who you are," he said, and fell into a moody silence.

A day or so later I had Katarina and Sally over for dinner—a cobbled together hasty meal of spaghetti and tomato sauce. I accidentally poured red wine into Katarina's glass of grapefruit juice. Katarina laughed, as did I, but Sally looked on guard, round brown eyes wide open.

"What have you been drinking?" she said. "You are completely smashed."

Later we went for a walk to look at the pulsating stars in the black night. It was, again, icy cold. Winter had returned, after that false spring. One day in early March I set off in the snow to meet Ruth, who was coming with me to Leida and Lydia's. She wasn't by the cowsheds as we'd agreed, but I eventually found her outside. As we ploughed through the snow towards the car she started to explain an Estonian point of grammar to me, precise and patient as ever. We reached the car and were on our way. Within a few minutes the wind picked up, and it started snowing again. Soon we were in a violent snowstorm, an actual blizzard. I drove cautiously on until Ruth said that we shouldn't continue, that the snowdrifts would be impassable nearer Einby. The storm, by then, felt actually dangerous, the wind whipping up deep drifts of snow on the road. Just after we turned we got stuck. Ruth got out to push, but to no avail. Snowflakes whirled across the windscreen. Eventually Ülo drove by and pushed us free. I tried to get Ruth to come home with me, but she sauntered off into the snow, with the cheese I had given her, casually waving a hand goodbye without turning her head.

*   *   *

Two days later, 8 March, was Virve's birthday, which coincided with International Women's Day, too associated with the Soviet Union to be celebrated anymore. I asked Alar what they used to do. "Flowers to the ladies," he said, smiling ironically. Laine made a speech in the teachers' room, both about Virve and Women's Day. Ivar made a speech, lost on most of us, about how really we should celebrate tomorrow instead, the hundredth anniversary of the founding of the German Social Democratic Party. Alar and the bus driver handed a flower to each woman from a pot on behalf of all the men, a post-Soviet ironic joke.

"Can you imagine," Katarina said, "I asked my students why they thought there was a Women's Day, and not one of them replied." Yet more proof for her of what a long way they had to go, rather than what a long way they had come.

Later in the evening we had a party for Virve. It followed its usual course. Alar told me about Veino. "The man with the dog," he said, and I remembered him as the fat man with a dirty straw-blond fringe, tiny dog on a leash. He was the only one who ever kept a dog on a leash. "This man," Alar said, "deals in vodka, any time, night or day, if you have a vodka problem go to him. He sells a big bottle for thirty kroons only." He looked at me expectantly, and I exclaimed politely.

He also told Katarina about a small shop that sold very cheap alcohol and cigarettes—a "black market shop," Katarina later called it.

"What do you mean a 'black market shop'?" I said. "There is no black market anymore."

"Oh, you know what I mean, where they dump the prices, smuggled goods . . ." She trailed off, and then changed the subject to the family packs of Swedish steel wool she had sent for, and which had just arrived. She had already polished the metal sink in her kitchen until it shone like a beacon.

Alar and Heli were always looking for a deal. They moved like fish in the water from shop to shop, looking for cheap deals. Only

once did I see them sad about shopping, which otherwise was satis-
fying for them, and that was when their son, Karl, suddenly started
to walk and needed shoes. They found out that the shoes cost 160
kroons in Haapsalu, far more than they could possibly afford.

"It's a *monopol*", Heli said sadly.

They decided they had to go to Tallinn to compare prices, or
even to Tartu because Tartu was cheaper than Tallinn.

The current of assimilation was tugging at me. At the same time,
reading my diary now, I see a recurring note of a crisis of meaning
underneath the mild struggle of everyday life. I heated water on the
wobbly stove for washing, I shopped and cooked (a little), I cleaned,
I taught. I felt almost constantly ill, with one thing or another. Just
getting by seemed to take up almost all my time. Spring, by now, was
really starting. The storks came back, and settled in their old nest by
the dairy. The snow was practically all gone, and after three warm
and sunny days the insect and bird life suddenly returned. Equally
suddenly, the children were outside again, playing and shouting in
the long twilight, until there was an almost deafening din echoing
between the blocks of flats. One day someone burnt the old brown
grass strewn with rubbish between the block, and the children kept
up their own private fires deep into the night.

There was an undercurrent, too, of something quite eerie about
that spring—something about feeling exposed after the deep privacy
of winter: hearing the children half sarcastically and half sweetly
call out long, drawn-out "haaalllloooos" after me; being woken at
three A.M. by sudden and violent knocks on my door, followed
by the sound of people running downstairs, laughing. They were
teasing me. I think now that they also knew more about me than
I thought—the anonymity I took for granted was, I think, gone
within weeks of my being there, maybe even earlier.

In the beginning I heard there was a rumour that I had taken
the name Rausing to conceal my identity of von Rosen, a descendant

of the former owners of the estate, who had left sometime after the first revolution of 1905. By a strange coincidence I had actually considered taking the name Rosen, conveniently similar, to conceal the identity of Rausing.

I didn't take another name in the end, and the von Rosen rumour didn't last long. I learnt later that they soon knew who I was and where I was from, but few people ever mentioned it. One day, an Estonian newspaper cutting about my family, in connection with some charitable donation, was posted on the noticeboard in the teachers' room. I surreptitiously removed it the same night, and because no one ever mentioned it again I almost forgot it. But I don't think they forgot it. They were just habitually discreet.

NINE

Normal Life

At the end of March I came back to the collective farm—I thought of it as "home" now—from a day in Tallinn. Veevi had been to Helsinki, to visit friends from before the war. She hadn't been there since that time. When I asked her how it was, she said it was quite "normal," and told me about an organisation of widows of artists her friend was involved in. She had seen exhibitions, gone to talks, taken in the culture. It was as "normal" as Tallinn was still "not normal."

I walked to the village of Österby that cold spring night, in the late lingering sunset and twilight, past the shadowy grey houses and the sketchy silhouettes of bare trees. Near Linnamäe, a stork flew over the field. There was a man and child in green boots on the road. The child climbed a milk stand, holding the man's hand. He had a cigarette in his mouth. They walked slowly past me.

Daniel Miller had encouraged me to write a synopsis of an "imaginary thesis" and send it to him, and I did, focusing on the signs of Swedishness in the village: "The public signs hint at a process by which the Swedish heritage is being re-appropriated and staged as a show inspired by a genuine wish to move towards the West, and a fear of isolation and impoverishment," I wrote, followed by an eleven-page outline. I had ten prospective chapters, with detailed notes, and a timetable. I sound so confident, until the end, when I added, "Please criticise as much as you want since it's all as liminal, transitional and uncertain as its subject."

Daniel wrote back. "Unlike conventional ethnography," he wrote, "you do not set a present against a represented past, but show a good sense of the historical conditions and present debates that not only construct new pasts today for measuring the present against, but also did so in the past with Swedish revivalist movements." It was hastily written, I understood that, and I knew what he was getting at. He wrote two more pages, gave me good suggestions for reading, and many comments, some of them critical: "Occasionally you get a bit too glib as in the idea of a symbolic drama in liminal stages of transition. I confess this did not appeal to me (but then I don't really like Turner)." I read his comments slowly, deciphering. It was the end of Turner, of course, but I wondered also if the whole of my imaginary thesis was too theoretical. I felt tired, and turned to my books, crammed onto the shelf next to Inna's glass animals. I counted them—124 books. Was it too many? I wondered. I already felt at times like I was merging into the identity of a teacher in the village, just trying to get by—was I also reading and writing too much, instead of "doing fieldwork"?

I needed more data. I visited Leida and Lydia, and asked if I could film them. Leida insisted, as a kind of return gift, informant to researcher, that I write down the Estonian Swedish version of the days of the Easter week: *Kråkmåndan, Krubbatisdan, Askonsdan, Skärtorsdan, Långfredan, Bakalaudan, Smaka Söndan.*

"Why *Kråkmåndan*," I asked, "like the crow?" Yes. "Why *Krubbatisdan*?"

"*Man kribbar omkring*—you *crib* around," said Lydia, and moved her arms like a crawling infant, with an indefinable expression on her face. She was making it up, of course—*krubba*, in fact, I later read, was a type of sausage, traditionally eaten at Easter. It is in the nature of humans to make things up, to create coherence and connections where there may be none.

They insisted, as usual, on giving me something real as well. First they tried to insist that I keep the change from the knitting needles I had bought for them. When I refused they said the change was payment for the passport photographs I had taken of them—Lydia had asked me if I could take her photograph since she was applying for a passport, and I had taken her photograph and sent the film to London to be developed, specifying that I needed four passport-sized photographs of the shot of her. Then they gave me a sweet, and insisted that I take the whole box. After that, they had a short consultation about what else they could give me, and whether the homemade pressed meat had set yet so that it was firm enough to give away. I refused, and said I had to go. There were to be no debts, there had to be balance—harmony, or perhaps equality.

Later I went for a walk, and was struck by the appearance of my footsteps in the snow and mud, showing the way back: surprisingly firm, pointing slightly outwards at the toes, moving steadily onwards. They were like an imagined, or submerged, alter ego, steady of purpose and decisive. I followed, trying to keep up like a child, breaking into half steps and trots, trying to fit foot into foot, backwards merging with forwards, an image, again, of my fieldwork. That night I dreamt about being a teenage runaway, dressed in a tight glittery top and a miniskirt. I was passing through a brothel, a large run-down flat where I was going to have to work as a prostitute; there were scantily dressed young women, dwarves and giants, a circus atmosphere. I ran past the women; they giggled, and moved closer together. I was not, in the dream, one of them—I was much younger, and quite scared. In the end I escaped through a window. There is a link, I see now, between the footprints in the snow, the two selves, and the strange alter ego in the dream: my sense of self was mildly splitting. Not into English and Swedish, as I had imagined it might, but a deeper split to do with agency and purpose versus submission. The footsteps out and the footsteps in. I was there out of my own free will, obviously, but sometimes it also felt like a sentence.

The next day I went over to Alar and Heli's. They were tired, and Karl, their toddler, had been ill. I gave them some clothes for him I had found in Tallinn, and a bottle of French brandy, cheap and unknown. Alar launched into a long story of how he'd bought some German whisky in Tartu that was undrinkable, like eau de cologne— "Like old eau de cologne," Heli interrupted, meaning Soviet eau de cologne, which people did drink, in the absence of vodka—and how he had complained to the Consumers' Organisation, which had rung the shop for the "quality control papers." The owner, an Indian, he thought, had said the shop could "make" the papers in an hour—Alar sneered—and the thing ended with Alar getting compensation (£2.50) and the shop being fined.

Whilst he told me this he was changing Karl, and I was getting increasingly worried about my own unknown bottle of VSOP brandy from Haapsalu. He started to ask me about what was good alcohol and what was bad. When I said I didn't know he asked how I could not know. And, of course, he was right—how could I not know? My pretence to not know was only a form of cultural relativism. I knew, for instance, that the brandy I had bought was probably not going to be very good, and that the shop where I had found it was not good either. It was what it was: an impulse buy. We had coffee, and he opened it and, to my relief, pronounced it to be "quite normal." Marika, the vet, came, and brought some buns.

Marika, their old friend, was in her mid-thirties, with long brown hair and a sensible face. Was she a single mother? I remember her that way, though I never saw her with her child, and she may not have been, but so many women were. We talked, that day, about Easter. I was startled by the fact that they knew nothing about the theology, not even the basic fact that Good Friday memorialises the crucifixion. Having grown up in an atheist home myself, it was the only time that I was really taken aback by the effects of Soviet atheism. I didn't otherwise notice the fact that there was no religious education in the school, no links to the church, no confirmations or marriages. I was too close to them, culturally, to find it remarkable.

Heli got an astrology book out, which warned us about possible burglaries. That amused them. Then we talked, or rather I talked, about the Russian coup rumours—they had heard nothing about it, and didn't care. We talked, also, about the Gloucester murderer, now long since forgotten, but big news then, and they told me of a serial killer in Ukraine, who had killed and eaten more than a hundred women. We talked about illness and peace, about Heli's alcoholic father and dyeing eggs with onion skin for Easter. Heli and Maris, her daughter, had rashes around their mouths, and I, too, developed the same unspecified rash.

The next day it rained steadily, and I stayed inside. Looking at people from the window, I realised that it was not easy to tell the women from the men. The vodka man, Veino, was jogging through the rain, little dog on a leash.

Soon afterwards I went back to Leida and Lydia's to film them. They talked to the camera about the people leaving for Sweden during the war, and how people from the east, Estonians from Russia, were resettled by the Germans in the area. I wondered what they thought of the newcomers. They were refugees, Leida said, who had lost everything: "They only cried, like us." She was in tears by now, as was Lydia. As I remember it, they had stayed behind when the other Swedes were evacuated because Lydia was too ill at the time, with polio. They talked more about the deportations, and the general fear of the knock on the door. There were never any letters, they said, from the people who had been arrested. No one knew what happened to them.

In 1953, after Stalin's death, there was a mass amnesty of mainly low-level prisoners from the Gulag. Most of them were released into internal exile, unable to come home, and were not exonerated. In 1956, following Khrushchev's famous speech denouncing Stalinism, "On the Personality Cult and Its Consequences," many more political prisoners were released. Some, but not all, were exonerated and rehabilitated. Many prisoners who had already been released into exile were also rehabilitated and allowed to go home. There were many posthumous rehabilitations, too.

Of the people who had been deported from the peninsula, only a few ever came back. The Soviet prisoners' stories of suffering and survival, of exhausted people dying of hunger and overwork, of eating grass and digging holes in the ground for shelter, never did become very public, even under Khrushchev. After his fall from power in 1964, orchestrated by Brezhnev and others, the hope of liberalisation gradually died away. There were no more mass deportations, but the history of the Gulag was suppressed, and it remained a risky topic of conversation. Political dissidents, of course, were still imprisoned or "treated" in mental hospitals, and many camps were kept open as prison colonies.

I remember the tears running silently down Lydia's cheeks. That video is lying in some dusty box now, I don't know where. Soon they started talking about the collective farm instead.

"In the beginning," Leida said, "people didn't want it." They associated it with the deportations. "But gradually it got a little better, and people got some pocket money, and cars and tractors started to come, and then people liked the *kolkhoz*." It was decades, however, before they were paid a wage. And the Russian troops? They laughed. "They were just nice boys like ours, far from home." They didn't mind them.

After we finished I showed them what we had recorded on the camera, using the earphones. They laughed out loud, Leida standing with her arms slowly waving like wings, rolling backwards and forwards on her feet. "What fun, what fun!" she said, and laughed. They thanked me sincerely, and suggested, again, that they should pay me. I was not surprised. I knew, also, that their monthly pension amounted to 280 kroon for Lydia (£14), and about 300 for Leida (£15). They might—just—have been able to afford to pay me 50 out of that, or £2.50. I refused.

School resumed after the Easter break. There was cabbage soup for lunch the first day. I had begun teaching voluntary French lessons. I also started to buy Polish washing-up liquid, a compromise improvement, and actually another sign of assimilation, but I stuck to Estonian washing powder. The day I abandoned that would be the day when I was no longer "doing fieldwork"; my position, then, would have become one of assimilation. The children played in the yard, slowly and aimlessly wandering about, hanging on the single swing. A little dog trotted past them, there were seagulls on the field beyond, and wood pigeons on the roof opposite.

I went for a walk through the fields that first school day, and came upon an abandoned house I had never seen before. I followed a mossy stone wall running next to an icy ditch deeper and deeper into a marshy part of the forest, ending up behind Ruth's cottage. I sat there for a long time, on a large stone in a meadow listening to the wind, watching the trees bend and the setting sun turn the grass deep green and golden. When I came back I turned on my old TV, which worked only intermittently. I was quite frightened to watch it; sometimes those old Soviet TVs exploded. There was music on, forceful and monotonous at the same time—the sound of Estonia.

By now I had gotten to know Tiina, whom I still thought of as the new teacher, quite well. She lived with her husband in another town, in an old house. A black stove heated the two rooms on the ground floor. She had no bathroom, but she did have a new microwave, an electric kettle, and a fridge. I visited her there, drinking German instant lemon tea. We talked about Rudolf Steiner and Célestin Freinet pedagogy in the warm sitting room with big plants, a slow and flea-ridden little Schnauzer puppy at our feet. Tiina did not comment on the flees jumping on his back, and neither did I. Outside the window, a meter or so away, was the house extension they were building. It looked like a stage set, the outside not really outside. Her kettle and fridge and microwave, too, made the house feel not quite real, the lack of a bathroom suddenly incongruous.

A few days later she took me to see her parents, who lived in a villa in Haapsalu, near the "Russian village." This was a strikingly different part of town: small wooden houses close together, rough and foreign, Russian looking.

"I don't understand it," she said, as Estonians always did, "how they want to live like that."

Haapsalu had a population of some fifteen thousand people. Two thousand Russians had already left for Russia. In the Soviet times it was a "closed" town because of the military installations. We drove past those later—camouflaged hangars surrounded by rusty barbed wire, still and abandoned. The military planes, her mother said, used to take off at four in the morning, and there were more stutterers in Haapsalu than anywhere else because of the noise and sleep disturbance. She also said that when the Soviet military left the troops saturated the ground with fuel, so that no planes could land ever again. I didn't know if that was true.

Her father was trying to learn English. He owned the *kaubahall*, the new supermarket, in Haapsalu. Inflation was now 50 percent he said, and interest on loans was 30 percent. I asked if that made business difficult. "No," he said, adding frankly, "But competition does."

The *kaubahall* was built in the in-between period and still seemed vaguely Soviet, as he did. He used to work in Narva, Leningrad, and Moscow, for a chemical engineering company making parts for the military. I asked what he thought of Boris Yeltsin. "I think he is a typical Russian," he said heavily, looking very much like Yeltsin himself. They had only two Russian neighbours now (their other Russian neighbours moved to Israel after Estonian independence), two families where the parents were deaf and dumb. There was a strange and tragic symbolism to this: that the only Russians living in the comfortable Estonian part of town were deaf and dumb, outside language, able to assimilate—or so I theorised—through their muteness.

We went to have lunch in the new Hotel Sport. The restaurant was quite good, new but aesthetically Soviet, like the *kaubahall*. There were few other customers, but the waitress still consistently brought the wrong things, which the family received patiently, in silence. She brought Cokes instead of orange juices, which they accepted. After some time she came back and asked whether we had asked for *kala* or *kana*—fish or chicken. Tiina and her parents politely explained that we had asked for fish. She was gone for a long time and then brought chocolate pudding instead of fish, which they actually sent back. It was all so new, somehow.

After our long lunch, we drove out to their summerhouse, a wooden hut built like a tent, the slanting roof reaching the ground. We went for a walk amongst the birches and juniper bushes and seagulls, down to the frozen sea, where some islands rose like mirages in the distance. Two white swans flew just above us, and their little brown dog, Monty, named after Jerome K. Jerome's terrier in *Three Men in a Boat*, leapt and ran about on the ice.

In mid-April the wind was still icy. There were days of power cuts, when the water supply, too, ground to a halt. I wrote about taste, about thrift, about cleanliness, normativity, and allegiances. One day I had my hair cut in the village, in a small room painted orange and white, with a basin in one corner, Finnish shampoo and hair spray on a shelf, and a hairdryer. A boy was having his hair cut when I arrived, then it was the turn of the school driver, and then it was my turn. Two children watched me closely as my hair was washed and cut in silence. Then it was dried, with some Finnish setting liquid, so that briefly I looked like my mother had in the 1970s, with an unflattering helmet of brown hair. I passed Katarina on the square outside, and she complimented me, seemingly in all sincerity, on my new haircut.

That month Ivar took a group of Swedes on a tour of Estonia, and I went with him. It was freezing cold in the early morning, but Ivar was, as ever, happy and energetic. We went to Viljandi, and saw the famous old oak on the ten-kroon note, and a monstrous six-storey piggery with room for twenty thousand pigs—it had not been a success, Ivar said. We went on to the Halliste Holy Anna Church, which had become a symbol for the new independence. A former collective farm director had become religious, and retrained as a vicar. The church had been struck by lightning in 1959, and he raised funds to restore it. Inside it was shoddy and icy. There was a large basement with vast and empty wardrobes, for concerts and so on. The brochure, published in 1990, stated it was built "For God, for the home, for the fatherland"—bad print on cheap paper. From there we drove to Pärnu by the sea, and a beach called Valgerand, "White Beach," which I accidentally directed us to. Since we were there, we stopped, and walked for a while. It was just after sunset. Huge blocks of ice were churned up together, with the blue sea beyond, a rind of uneven ice above the horizon like a floating island.

The following day the Swedes met to discuss community development in the village. Ain Sarv, editor of *Ronor*, and the director of a new Swedish adult education college, a modest development dedicated to educating people about Estonia's Swedish heritage, was there, as were Laine and Felix Sedman. Ivar chaired the meeting. Ülo was going to be there, but was absent, which was just as well given his recent clash with Felix. Aime Sügis, an MP for whom Toivo occasionally worked, was there, too. She was a woman in her sixties, dignified and intelligent, who ran a "health school" on the peninsula. The meeting was entitled "Perspectives on the Development of the Council." Local entrepreneurs and "organisers" had been invited, too, but only two people bothered to respond, and no one turned up. Ivar spoke first. The gist of his talk was that just over half the people working on the peninsula did so without paying any tax. We learnt, also, that the last three-year plan for the community, which was agreed to in 1991, had six aspects: to foster Swedish culture; to support small-scale farming, shooting, environmentalism, and tourism; and to encourage potato farming. Laine, scribbling incomprehensibly on the board, talked about the discussions in 1989 about Noarootsi as a cultural centre: the Estonian Swedish museum in Haapsalu, the Society of Swedish Estonian archives (then housed in Ivar's home), the library, the Paslepa adult education school, and the health school, she added, as an afterthought, acknowledging Amie. She added sadly that it was a pity that the museum was in Haapsalu and not here.

Amie then talked about her health school. It was started seven years ago for "health and development." It charged 200 kroons a week, and the students worked in the garden and kitchen. They advised farmers on health and organic agriculture; on life philosophy; on how to think, breathe, and eat; on stress; and on plant use. The students slept in the attic and in tents. Amie herself slept in the sauna. I couldn't look at Ivar, who was now enough of a friend to laugh with—the thought of the farmers I had met taking advice on how to think, breathe, and eat was too funny.

Now it was the turn of the Swedes. One of them proposed creating a tourist village by the sea.

"Well, someone would have to build it," Ivar said, before launching into a tirade about the unemployed in the village, so disorganised, so decadent, so alcoholic.

Another Swede, slightly disapproving of Ivar's tone, suggested study circles to help the unemployed.

"They won't come," Ivar said. "They'd rather drink."

The Swedes looked uncomfortable.

"They don't just drink," Felix Sedman said in his deep voice, "they are drinking themselves to death."

They were, I think, playing with the Swedes, but at the same time, the struggle with drink actually was the most important social issue on the peninsula. Casual labour was divided into drinkers and nondrinkers, and the latter were paid more, as a matter of course. Österblom's struggle against alcoholism on Ormsö, and Nymann and Pöhl's temperance society in Noarootsi, had been long since forgotten. The only temperance discussion, other than the above, that I ever heard on the collective farm was when Mart Niklus, the former dissident and MP, visited. He wouldn't drink vodka, which he associated with the brutality of the guards of the labour camp where he was incarcerated for sixteen years. Apart from him, everyone drank, even Ivar, and Felix Sedman was right: many people, mostly men, were drinking themselves to death.

At this time two friends from England, Tara and Karen, came out for a visit, and we travelled by car through Estonia and down to Latvia. First we visited Paldiski, the Russian military base. The first checkpoint we came to was manned by a Moldovan, a small man with a black moustache, tunic open, who came hurrying out after he'd seen us take pictures. We had a reasonably friendly conversation with him, whilst his brutal-looking sidekick stood leaning against the door of the hut. When we left, he called us back to ask for cigarettes, and would only take two although Karen offered him a whole packet. We drove on through the town, past the unrenovated high-rises, trees lining the road, Russian troops walking by.

The next checkpoint was guarded by a single Estonian, and I asked if we could look around. He asked somebody else over the intercom system, and the permission came out loud and crackly, improbably in tune with the surroundings. The barracks, once solid, perhaps even beautiful, were now completely dilapidated. The Estonian soldier showed us around as if he hadn't seen the inside of the buildings himself, curiously looking into every room. The assembly room, about thirty meters long, was supported by pillars covered in a coarse mosaic depicting the themes of the Soviet nations—it was like finding the archaeological remains of a past empire. Other rooms had broken chairs and rusty beds in them, and old Soviet frescoes on the walls gradually merging with the background colour. The exercise ground was outside the barbed wire of the camp, full of rusty structures, some covered in rotting cloth; a war aesthetic.

Leaving the base, we followed the dirt road, and eventually reached the harbour. A Russian war ship was leaving the dock. Armed soldiers stood on board watching the shoreline recede. The sea was rainbow with fuel, and an Estonian soldier on a bicycle was idly watching the ship go out. That was the last we saw of Paldiski, and we left by a dirt road that led all the way back to Rickul and Noarootsi. Whilst we were still on the mainland, a young elk, heavy and clumsy, cantered across the road right in front of us on uncertain legs.

The next morning we drove to Pärnu, and then on to Riga. We drove down dusty wide boulevards, looking at house facades with dramatic and artistically painted adverts, children begging, and men looking at us appraisingly. We parked outside the hotel. A man in worn-out clothes and small green eyes in a tired face, asked us for money for the parking, mentioning the Mafia, and the need to protect the car against attacks, when we hesitated. We paid up.

The Russian church in Riga, which had been partially turned into a planetarium in the Soviet era, was being restored. The icons, which had been left, were still covered with a patina of grime and dust. Outside, children were begging next to bent old women in dirty grey headscarves. The main boulevard led up to a blue high-rise, the Hotel Latvija, multicoloured strings of lights in the trees lining the road. The Russian on the formerly bilingual street signs had been roughly painted over with grey paint. Our destination, a synagogue on a back street, was closed, and instead we went to the top of a church tower. The fencing at the top was rusty and unsafe. We stood there, looking out over Riga. It really was another country.

The next day we drove out to Salaspils, the former concentration camp set in the eternal pine forests of the Holocaust. The camp was demolished long ago, and in 1969 it was turned into a Soviet monument. Some fifty thousand people were killed there, Jews and Soviet prisoners of war. There was a stone memorial of huge, gaunt figures. In front was a dark, low slab of stone, a steady echoing sound emanating from it, like a prison door swinging in the wind: the symbolic time keeping of the camp. There were some sodden flowers on the stone. A man cycled slowly across the camp, a shortcut to the village, perhaps. It was a grey rainy day. Shockingly, *JUDEN RAUS* graffiti in the primitive lavatories.

Estonia seemed so mild and idyllic, so comforting, in comparison with Latvia. We stopped in Tartu, the university town, and had dinner in a restaurant with an enormously formal waiter. A woman was playing the piano in a dilapidated house, window open to the blue evening. She turned towards us as we passed. The old university buildings reminded me a little of the Swedish university town of Lund, where I grew up. It was quiet and peaceful. We must have stayed somewhere along the way, but I have no memory of that now, and no note of it in my diary. Coming back to the collective farm the next morning felt like coming home. There was Alar and Heli, and Karl, the toddler, in a harness being walked. Katarina, in improbably ugly orange sunglasses, came over to say hello. Sally, much recovered from a reclusive spell, came for a visit later. I was happy to be back.

Soon after this trip I started to give English lessons for adults. As my students left, I would hear them call to each other "bye-bye," laughing. I knew them all. Eve from the post office, who took it more seriously than anyone else, had been almost in tears with frustration about pronunciation. I recognised her frustration only too well from my own Estonian lessons. I had never before had the sense that English was difficult to pronounce, I suppose because I always heard it so much, but for them it was different. In Estonian pronunciation is predictable from the spelling, and they found the gap between what they read and what they heard in English difficult. Also, in Estonian, the exact pronunciation determines both meaning and case form: unlike English, it's not a forgiving language. I told Eve that a global language has so many different accents that pronunciation inevitably matters less than in Estonian, but I don't think she believed me.

On the eve of Mayday there was the dress rehearsal for lighting the midsummer fires. I waited for an hour and a quarter in the rain for the bus with Ivar and a friend of his, Allan, the director of the historical museum in Haapsalu. Allan was researching the bureaucracy of the Soviet mass deportations in 1941 and 1949. He had, as I remember it now, studied history with Ivar at Tartu, and they had remained friends. The rehearsal was chaotic and elemental, a huge fire in the rain, spits of flame whipped up by the gusts of wind shooting towards the sea.

Later, wet through, we went back to Ivar's flat. I hadn't seen it before. It was unexpectedly beautiful, with stripped dark wood and orderly bookcases with interesting titles, books that looked read. I remember dancing by myself waiting for them to come back from the bar to get a bottle of vodka. More aware than I was of how much people gossiped in the village, Ivar didn't want me to come with them to buy it. Then we played roulette on a flimsy cardboard set. Ivar won three times in a row, decisively whirling the little plastic wheel.

In May I went to England for a week to see my mother, who had broken her ankle. I flew back into Tallinn, and retrieved my car. A tanned elderly man in the hut by the parking field slowly counted up the days I'd been away. Standing there on the wooden steps in the sunshine, I was struck again by the peace of Estonia.

I slowly drove back to Pürksi, little Ladas gliding past each other barely accelerating, the sun beating down, a hallucinatory shimmer on the road. I stopped at the ruins of the great manor house about an hour outside Tallinn, and walked around for a while. I had been there with Leigh before—this time it looked not so much tragic and beautiful as sad and dirty. There was a pile of broken bottles on one side, and the park behind the house, which had looked magnificent in its decline, now looked scruffy. It was peaceful nonetheless, with an unpretentious *kolkhoz* living block right in front, and a few vegetable plots on the left. Some people were standing around, talking, looking, and then not looking.

For moments I was taken aback that I understood exactly what they were saying. This had started already in London, when two Estonian women had boarded the plane in front of me. They were casually chatting—". . . and of course this was my first time in London . . ."—and I understood everything. Briefly, it felt like having been given the magical power of understanding birdsong, understanding what I intuitively felt I shouldn't, the banality of another world, beneath the exotic veneer of otherness. It was as if I had expected that that week in England would have robbed me of everything to do with Estonia, taking away all the insights, memories, knowledge, and ideas. It was, after all, so strange, so different from my normal life, to be there, on that collective farm in the former Soviet Union. So strange and yet so normal, so very ordinary.

At the same time, on the collective farm I often feared that I would forget my time in England, and, particularly, that my English would gradually disappear. I was sinking back into something like Swedishness, a Swedishness as foreign as my own, and therefore paradoxically familiar. Most people on the collective farm were not Swedish, but the people who were searched for words in the same way I sometimes did. We had in common that we were minorities, fluent in the majority language, mother tongue hidden inside us.

I stopped off to do some shopping on the mainland, and that, too, was pleasantly familiar: an unsmiling young man holding out a basket for me, scrubby women and red-faced men, spare and thrifty purchases, quick queues. Later I saw Sally on the square. She was unexpectedly tanned, and told me she had decided to leave. No surprises there. I saw Katarina, too, who now had short hair, a blond helmet like my dark one, but otherwise looking much the same.

The light was intense, almost a pure white. There were flowers and greenery all around. Already I missed the bleakness of early spring, the sketchy silhouettes of the trees against twilight evenings, the pallor and fragility of the April light. That night I went for a walk late in the evening, after eleven, and it was still dusky, with the remains of a pale orange sunset, the moon a full quarter by the evening star, a mist over the low-lying fields. Standing on the road listening to the cacophony of birds, echoing like in a jungle, thinking about the sound of dinosaur worlds, a stork flew past me on its way to the nest on the chimney of the old dairy.

That night I had a dream: I was walking on a savannah at sunset. It was improbably beautiful, as though dusted with gold. I was watching a pair of eagles slowly circling in the sky; I knew they were enormously rare. I saw them descend towards a pit, their home, and I walked towards them. Two British birdwatchers were hiding nearby, wiry and bespectacled observers with binoculars. They beckoned me over, whispering that I had to be very quiet. The two birds were standing now. They hadn't seen us. I was struck by their ordinariness; they were bird-people, but the bird-woman's hair was bleached and permed, forming a strange contrast to the extraordinary beauty and exoticism of the vision of them slowly circling. It was a man and a woman, and they had human bodies, naked, with eagle wings folded, but also tied on, behind their arms. They were a parallel species, not quite human.

It struck me that this dream was about my fieldwork: the grandeur of the theoretical framework, the extraordinary beauty of the country, the spectators with their lenses, the levels of theoretical interpretation, and the ordinary poverty of life in the village.

After no BBC World Service for eight months, I turned the radio on to hear a snatch of dialogue: ". . . and how much does one of these cost?" "Five pounds." "And it's small enough to carry away in a pocket, isn't it?" "Yes, it is." And then the voices faded out again. From my window I could see small children playing by themselves in the yard, unaware of being observed, leaning on the swing, investigating the ground, turning and trotting down the little path that cut off a corner of the grassy patch. The swallows and house martins dived and played in the wind, a door banged, a draught moved through the room.

Katarina and I went to the church service for Ascension Day. There were twenty-nine women in the congregation, mostly elderly, and a single elderly man. The church was white and a mild grey green, with irregular windows. The central aisle was made of broad flagstones, and the high-backed benches were constructed from painted grey planks. The service was given by a Finnish pastor, pale and ardent, his sermon translated into Estonian by an Estonian pastor. Katarina, objecting, as ever, to symbolic and complex arrangements, whispered, "Can you understand why they come here? It seems so unnecessary, if you see what I mean."

I was thinking of other things. We were praying, and I looked at the Bible, published by the Estonian church in exile in cooperation with the Estonian church in Canada in 1991. I read some passages, and listened to the prayers, thinking of the Anglican prayer: "We are not worthy so much as to gather up the crumbs under thy table . . ." I thought of the taste of the wine, the crucifix, and the old model ship hanging from a beam in the Norman church where

I first heard those words. I looked down at the drops of paint that had fallen on the rough plank floor under the pews. They seemed to symbolise something about Christianity at its best, a humility that is not false, a humanity and simplicity.

A younger woman, Eve, came over to speak to us afterwards. She was a friend of Amie Sügis, the MP from the health school whom I had already met. Writing this now, it occurs to me how many people had the same name on the collective farm. There was Inna, my first landlady, and Inna, the second one. There was Inna's Toivo, and Toivo the gamekeeper. There was also, confusingly, Alar the English teacher, and Allan the museum director; Veevi in Tallinn, and Virve in the village; Eve who ran the post office, and the Eve we met at the church. The latter Eve invited us back with her to visit Amie's health school, a new building, heated by wood stoves. I was interested to see it, so we went with her. She also showed us the garden and told us about the organic pesticides, gesticulating precisely, her intense blue eyes shining, invigorating and cheerful.

Afterwards we went on to Eve's own home, a house built in 1972, with a thatched roof and an old stove in the kitchen. She had five children. The older son was carrying his baby sister around like a parcel, the baby gurgling and grimacing. In the kitchen a man— whom I assumed to be her husband—was eating mashed potatoes and cabbage out of a tin bowl with bread and milk. Eve cut us each a piece of the unsalted bread; it crumbled like cake in my hand. The children watched, the man ate in silence, and Eve talked and talked. Outside two heifers licked our hands with long grey tongues. A little calf, removed from its mother, rested nearby. There were hens crowded into a dirty enclosure, and a fat grey cat that came running when Eve called. There was a telephone, too, sitting on the steps of the house.

Later she took us along to Amie's house, an old log house that had been pulled down and rebuilt in the 1920s. A thin man with a washed-out moustache was sitting at the table eating dry potatoes from a tin bowl. Sügis herself was in bed in the other room, exhausted by a bout of fasting. She was lying on three pillows under an embroidered shawl, cheeks red, eyes blurred, but she was lucid and coherent. We talked about the house, her experiments with organic pesticide, and the school. There was such a strange juxtaposition of old-fashioned poverty, self-imposed fasting, the quiet struggle of farming, and organic ideology there.

I had been curious about her for some time. Toivo, I knew, had a gripe with her because she hadn't paid him for some work he had done and, adding insult to injury, had told Inna what to feed the children ("Estonian vegetables"). After our conversation, Eve took us around the garden, and showed us the old sauna and the fields beyond the house. A young woman in a cardigan was spreading earth over seed potatoes in the cold wind.

It was spring, and the visitors were returning like migrating birds. On the way back we met some returning Swedes, a woman of about sixty with snow-white hair, and two men in a Volvo. One of the men told me his life story, of orphanages, foster homes, and the sea. The woman spoke Estonian with Eve in that particular Swedish accent, neutralising all the clipped consonants and the drawn-out vowels. This was my family home, she said, pointing to a derelict log house by the side of the road.

We went on to visit Irma, a Swedish old lady, a relative of Eve's. The conversation was halting. Eve, nursing the baby on the bed in the corner, couldn't quite understand why—she kept looking eagerly from one of us to the other, making encouraging signs. She didn't know that we had met before, and that Irma then had declined to be interviewed for my fieldwork, and that we were now both embarrassed by that. She eventually brought out a box of photos, a mix of old black-and-white portraits, colour snapshots with various Swedish relatives, as well as a few pictures from relatives in Sweden, outside and inside their ordinary comfortable Swedish homes. The photos looked strange in this cottage, which couldn't have changed much since the war, with its iron bedstead, table, and two chairs.

"They have a good life over there," she said, and laughed a little bitterly.

She took us outside to see her cows. Two were hers, and one she had received from the *kolhoos* herd when it was broken up. She had two calves as well, kept in a dirty pen, one of them slow and unwell. "Are you a bit poorly?" she said to the sick one, but he only bent his head and stood still.

She offered me a sauna then. It was still warm, she said. It was, in fact, only lukewarm, but there was some hot water in a bucket and a small piece of brown soap. She got me a towel and two birch branches to whip myself with, which I did half-heartedly, until I saw a green translucent little creature walking unsteadily across my thigh.

Sitting in that sauna I thought of forms of knowledge—concrete knowledge like how to milk a cow or dye eggs with onion skin, and experiential knowledge like the scent of the birch leaves in the sauna, spicy and strong. I thought, also, of the accumulation of meaning, and the images that lay behind the words of poverty: wood stoves, small iron beds, old clothes, sores around the mouths of children, tin buckets with water, old pieces of brown soap, potatoes and cabbage. The vodka of hardship, lined dark faces, glazed eyes, clothes melting onto the body, dirty hands red and cut. Those words are so meaningful if you have seen the reality of it, and lived with it, and so empty if you have not. And now, so many years later, the meaning is gradually leaching out of the words. I am forgetting.

TEN

Everything Is Wonderful

Katarina's birthday was at the end of May. We sang for her in English and in Estonian at school. I gave her dinner—tinned mussels from Sweden in a white wine and cream sauce, substituting Russian champagne for the wine, and soft cheese for some of the cream, which was past its sell-by date in the shop. Katarina talked about being pregnant and having children.

"Of course I worked the whole time—we do in Sweden—but it was lovely. You never regret having children. You can't because once they are born they are there, and you love them automatically."

There was a cold, dry wind and a glaring light outside, even late in the evening. Midsummer, and the white nights, were approaching.

We visited the island of Saaremaa with its medieval town, Kuressaare. The little town was startlingly neat and tidy. Even the woodpiles were neatly stacked, sometimes in pleasant decorative patterns, and the old co-op shop had all the goods stacked and lined up to the millimeter. We were staying with an old work friend of Inna's, an ambulance driver, from the time she worked as a dispatcher in Pärnu. When we finally arrived we were given dinner, by which time Katarina and I were so hungry we'd spent the latter half of the journey making up menus, an old childhood game of my father's. The dinner was delicious—*kotlet* with potatoes, and two kinds of pickles. There was a conformity about Estonian food that mirrored other conformities: the language with its set phrases used again and again, the flats with their ever-present wall units and sofas, the collective farms themselves, the clothes, the styles, the looks. Variety came mainly from want: the inability to keep up, clothes kept together with pins, dirty hair, the stale air of poor flats.

Inna's friend, whose name I now can't remember, was tall, angular, and humorous, very much a contrast to Inna, so round and brown with sad eyes. She lived with her son and Belarusian daughter-in-law—they had met at marine college in Russia. There was a black-and-white photograph of them in the front room, two thickset blond people with flared jeans looking gravely into the camera, standing very near each other, on a street with tall white houses in the background—not, I think, in Estonia. Now they had two little girls, looked after by their grandmother.

The house was built in 1974. They built it themselves, without a flushing lavatory, and with washing facilities only in the sauna, from a cold tap behind a curtain, though they did get around the regulations to make it a bit bigger than it should have been. There was a large garden, too, half of it a vegetable plot. They had chicken and pigs, a small dog, and a huge black Newfoundland, young and excessively friendly. He had no papers, Inna's friend said, but some experts had come to look at him, and were going to write out a certificate authenticating his breed. The small dog, scruffy and full of fleas, was chained; the Newfoundland, Cherry, slept outside the sauna at night. Large bones were scattered around the garden. The little girls ran up to Cherry, hugging him and shouting endearments in his ear as he stood stock-still, tail sinking.

Later we went for a cold but wonderful walk. The sun was setting over an inlet, the castle stood dark and solid in the background, the streets were quiet. The old wooden houses with carved verandas were so beautiful in the blue evening light. Cats lying on the woodpiles watched us as we walked by, overtaken by old people riding slowly past on rusty bicycles. There was music coming from the windows of run-down houses; children were playing in the streets.

The next day we went for a drive. We passed two houses, yards untidy and unkempt. "Look at that," said our host, as so many Estonians had said to me. "That is how the Russians live."

We stopped at a lake, where I swam, alone, in the cold clear water. Our destination was an old farm, now a museum. The previous farmer, according to a pamphlet in English, had "agreed to assign most of the ethnographical necessaries preserved in the farm to the state free of charge." That was in 1959. "The first worker of the museum was Jakob Reht (the farmer in question) who until his death in 1969 kindly acquainted the guest with the exposition of the farm." Afterwards we saw the church and some shops, similar to the two shops in Pürksi, and then we had coffee in a Soviet-style café. The others had coffee and cake; I had a "pizza," a small, round, faintly rancid disk. There was only us and two drunk men. They got up as we did, walking unsteadily down the main street.

On the way home we saw a hedgehog hurrying across the street. "What is it called in English?" asked Inna, and I was just going to say the word, when I realised I couldn't remember. I knew it had something to do with pigs, but all my mind would come up with was "guinea pig." I was in between going blank and simply having forgotten. I knew I would know it instantly if I was told, but I also felt a deeper sense of alienation that made me think of my relationship to English as a secondary, learnt language: at some point I must have consciously learnt the word "hedgehog" from the Swedish word *igelkott*, and at some point later I must have transferred the sense of congruity between the animal itself (the signified) and the word (the signifier) from Swedish to English, from *igelkott* to "hedgehog." Now they both feel possible: *igelkott* playful and poetic, "hedgehog" more prosaic but also somewhat more descriptive. *Igelkott* is a smaller, blacker, and wetter image than hedgehog, the inside more than the outside; a snail more than a pig.

I slept intermittently that night, and dreamt heavily. Before we left the next morning, I looked at a book on the table, on Soviet Estonian art, in English:

> The turning point in the evolution of artistic thought, the ebbs and flows of creation are all connected in highly complicated ways with the crucial points of history. It might be difficult to find art events which, if aligned in a chronological sequence would correspond to the critical dates of the last forty-five years. But there still is a connection. It lies deeper than a row of dusty archives dates. It is the mental connection. As a sensitive measuring device, art reacts to the changes in the spirit of society, recording what is new and at the same time trying to compensate for deficiency . . .
>
> Those were complicated years. A number of things were not understood, and many things were misunderstood. But those were the contradictions that are inevitably typical of every progressive movement.

Soviet texts were always hypocritical and comforting in equal measure, comforting in the same way that the school books were comforting: cheerful and coherent; a facade of good intent; the cotton-wool reality of censorship.

At the end of May a rumour went around the village that Sally had disappeared. We knocked on her door, often, and looked for her. It didn't occur to any of us to call the police—I had never seen any police on the peninsula. Several days later she emerged, startled by the attention. She had been there all the time, in retreat. She invited me for coffee, and talked about the book she was writing, about Canada, about being a librarian, and about being here. She had randomly picked up this teaching job, I can't remember how, and come over without any connection to Estonia, or an organisation like the Peace Corps. Her flat, similarly, was untouched; she lived so lightly in it. As I stood in the door to leave, she casually picked up a broom and brushed some dust under the rug in the hallway. I looked on in fascination—I had never imagined I would see anyone actually brush dust under the carpet. The act seemed to live on only as an expression of concealment, but here it was. "Oh, I do it all the time," she said, laughing. "It doesn't matter, does it?"

The next day was the birthday of the school cook. Unlike the teachers' birthdays, always celebrated with a full quorum of teachers, cake, and coffee, her birthday was only casually celebrated. She came to the teachers' room, tall and heavy, her face red and eyes slightly bleary. We didn't sing, though we did eat cake, and everyone shook her hand. She was not, I noted, drunk. It was a grey and windy day. It seemed that every day then was windy. Two women were working on the field behind the block of flats opposite mine, bending down, moving slowly over the earth. Shortly afterwards Katarina got an acute toothache. I asked Ivar about the dentist, and he said that there was no dentist here.

"How odd," I said, "since the Åtvidaberg correspondence shows that dentistry equipment was sent. Asked for, actually."

"Yes, but it would be too expensive to have a dentist here. There's not enough need."

The dentistry equipment was lost, I assumed, sold or stored somewhere. Katarina went to Haapsalu instead, and a dentist there pulled out her tooth, without any anaesthetic. She was brave like that.

In the beginning of June Sally left, and so did Katarina. Sally gave me her Cowboy Junkies tape, appropriately haunting. I spent an hour fixing my leaky piping under the sink with some duct tape she had also given me—it half worked. She had adopted a white cat. It was now at a loose end, searching for food by the rubbish bins. Soon after they left, midsummer arrived and, with it, the revived tradition of a midsummer bonfire. We had rehearsed for this, in a howling rainstorm, and now, again, there was a storm. The huge fire was so beautiful, whipped by the wind and the rain, the stormy sea in the background.

The evening before Toivo, the gamekeeper on the peninsula, had asked me to go and have a *shashlik* (a Russian kebab) with him in the bar by the harbour, of roe deer he'd shot himself. I had met him before, when I conducted my survey, flat by flat. He was kind, I remembered, explaining words I didn't know, making sure I really understood what he meant. Unlike most people in the village, he had black hair and a black beard, and deep brown eyes. I had been filming a Swedish midsummer event when he asked me. The choir sat on the stage waiting for something or other. I killed a mosquito landing on my cheek. The fire was pointlessly turning into coal, and I was feeling bored. He was standing behind me with two men. They ostentatiously and courteously backed away as I swung the camera around. I smiled, and Toivo came over at once, talkative, friendly. As he turned to go I saw that he was hiding a crushed can of Gin Long Drink in his hand.

I went with him to the bar in his pickup truck. We had a beer. His children came in, with wildflowers for me, for midsummer. I refused a second beer: the evening was too thick with atmosphere already. We left earlier perhaps than we otherwise would have done, and went for a drive up the coast on the small dirt roads. It was cold then, and the wind was strong. At one point we drove past three dead cows lying in a heap, swollen and brown. My mouth dried up, looking at them. He had told me about three deaths earlier: his newborn baby, and two friends who had died in Afghanistan. He winced exactly like his namesake Toivo, my landlord, used to: a movement of the mouth, and an incongruous thumbs-up. "That's life," he said. "It happens." Stoic, and brief.

As he dropped me off outside my building, he kissed me on the cheek, our cheekbones knocking together. I went to my flat, the possibilities of another life tugging, as ever. At midsummer it was never fully dark. Late at night in the dimming light I went for a long walk. I saw an elk, that mysterious heavy being, crashing into the forest, and then a roe deer. I picked seven kinds of wildflowers in a private Swedish midsummer ritual to put under my pillow. As I got back there was an almost full moon hanging above the *kolkhoz* workshop, a streak of black cloud across it. A black cat was roaming amongst the rubbish bins, a seagull sailing overhead. Everything was quiet.

The midsummer flowers are meant to make you dream of your future husband. Instead I dreamt about Toivo's wife. She came down the staircase from Sally's, where she had been working in a laundry, and greeted me with a friendly smile; one of those dream sequences that are so real that they are hard to distinguish from actual memories.

The morning after that I saw Toivo from my window carelessly stepping out on the roof of the two-story block of flats at a right angle to mine. He walked halfway down the steep side, with nothing to hold on to and not even a gutter to grab should he stumble, and waved at me from the roof.

I was copying a video I had made for Virve at Alar and Heli's. Karl was sleepless, hot and restless. I pressed the top of a perfume bottle against his nose and he laughed, and then pressed his nose against it again and again. They were tired and quiet. We talked about the speech I had made to the group of diplomats who had visited the village. Laine had asked me to speak, together with one of the students, and some of the teachers, but she had made it clear afterwards that she wasn't very happy with what I had said.

"I didn't know what to say. Maybe it wasn't right, but what should I have said?" I asked Alar and Heli.

"That everything is all right, everything is wonderful," said Alar, smiling ironically.

This is what I said:

"The fall of the Soviet Union led to a strong wave of interest from social anthropologists. The concurrent critique of Marxism led to questions about how to describe societies—or communities —which had, at least partially, and for a long time, described themselves in terms of dialectical Marxism, at a time when those terms were rapidly becoming redundant. There was a movement, therefore, towards fieldwork in the former nations of the Soviet state, in order to investigate the practises of everyday life. I was interested in this because of the possibilities of combining history and anthropology; of trying to write social anthropology, which would take the various historical trajectories into account.

"This region seemed well suited for the project, in that there was a strong historical component in the form of the culture of the Estonian Swedes. This culture, which was intensely investigated from Sweden in the twenties and thirties, to the point where it was ironically said that every Estonian Swede had become an ethnographic object, is now to some extent going through a second wave of investigation, both from Sweden and from Estonia. There are local attempts to revive the Swedishness—I am thinking both about this school, and the *Paslepa Folkhögskola,* and the Society of Estonian Swedish Culture, *Samfundet för Estlandssvensk Kultur.* These attempts constitute, I would argue, both an attempt to reconnect the area with the history of the first republic, bypassing the Soviet era, and an attempt to forge out a future built on these links.

"The majority of the Estonian Swedes, as I am sure you know, fled to Sweden during the war. The ones who remained became largely assimilated, and certainly the generations after them became almost entirely assimilated. The present schoolchildren, however, learn Swedish, and a degree of what you might call Swedishness, at school, and whilst this doesn't constitute a process of deassimilation, it might be described as an experiment in reinventing culture. The driving force, however, behind the restoration of Swedishness is not so much a resurrection of the past for its own sake, but rather a process of building a future which is not based on the Soviet past.

"The link with the Swedish town of Åtvidaberg, which is now twinned with Noarootsi, has resulted in a large amount of aid, mostly clothes and machinery, estimated to exceed a million Swedish crowns, or some hundred thousand pounds. There are also a number of other links with Swedish and Swedish Estonian organisations, as well, of course, as a large number of Swedish Estonian visitors from Sweden, coming back to see their childhood homes. What they see is rather poignant: the old farms, which tend to be run-down or even completely dilapidated; the council blocks built on what used to be an open field behind the old manor house; and the rusty workshops on the other side.

"This is the aesthetic of the material culture of the Soviet era, which is not so easy to get rid of, and which also reflects the fact that the people in the council blocks are mostly former *kolkhozniks*, who now see an uncertain future of poverty and unemployment, and who don't tend to participate in the project of the restoration of Swedishness, which largely takes place within the premises of the school and the local council. They tend to work for the new share-companies, which come and go, or else get by from job to job. These people have, of course, become 'free' with the fall of the Soviet Union, but a large number of them have also become 'redundant,' in the widest sense of the word.

"Anthropologists don't tend to deal with the future, just as they don't tend to deal with the past. The present here, however, is so entirely framed both by the past and the future that it almost doesn't exist. There is a sense in which people are waiting for the future to happen, stocking up as far as they can against a sense of uncertainty which represents both the actual condition of poverty and the loss of the teleology of the Soviet ideology: that pervasive sense of working towards a goal, which also, of course, was part of the great deception of the state. The Soviet modernity, meanwhile—the modernness of the then nice blocks of flats, the gigantic machinery on the enormous fields—is decidedly over. Equally, however, the pre-war aesthetic of the milk stands along empty dusty roads, and what might be described as the *heimat* worldview of thrift, order, and belonging, is over, too. In my view the challenge is how to build a future from the violent rupture of the Soviet years without further marginalising the people, who are involuntarily stuck in a quasi-Soviet aesthetic, which can now be reframed simply as poverty."

One of the French diplomats came up to me afterwards. "But your English is very good," he said, surprised. "Do you come from this area?'

Everybody wore summer clothes except me—I had nothing cooler than jeans and a T-shirt. It was very hot by now, a heatwave that was to last the whole summer. I walked, read, wrote, and continued my survey. I had reached the poor end of the village, long blocks of flats built in the early 1960s with serrated metal stoves for heating, and wood-fired ranges in the kitchen. The people in those flats were a little different—things seemed to have changed less here. The people were not all Estonian either. I interviewed a Tartar woman and an Uzbek man; she spoke some Estonian, he didn't. Russian was disappearing from Estonia, and this man was gradually becoming trapped in a language he didn't understand and had little hope or inclination to learn. There was one Russian woman left in the village, and she lived here. She, also, spoke no Estonian, but her neighbours began to translate for me. In the end we all laughed, because she spoke so much, and so quickly. I came back in the evening, and her husband, a big Estonian with a beard and bare chest, answered all my questions again, slowly and precisely.

An eighteen-year-old Estonian Swedish girl in that block sat peacefully knitting throughout the interview. She had blue-grey eyes clear like glass, and spoke Swedish in a low, slightly gravelly voice, searching for words, but well. Her father was from Ormsö, the island owned by the Swedish Baron von Stackelberg, which the Swedish missionary Österblom had lifted out of alcoholic poverty. Her father had kept his Swedish identity, and as a result he was not allowed in the Pioneers, the Soviet youth organisation. She and her brother had also identified as Estonian Swedes. She had decided already as a child that she wanted to be Swedish.

I asked why she said there were so many people here who were "actively Russian," meaning Soviet-minded Estonians. The Swedish high school started in 1990, and she was a border in the first year. I asked what was different in the beginning. "We had a lot of contact with the villagers then," she said, "especially the ones who like to start the day with fifty grams of vodka." Now that was not the case anymore. The high school students were, on the whole, slightly contemptuous of the villagers; they were seen as provincial, alcoholic, promiscuous, and lazy. The poor were increasingly marginalised. The alcoholics sat on the wide windowsill of the old shop, glassy-eyed and red-faced, quietly drinking.

That night I walked towards the old dairy. The pine trees shivered in the wind against what was left of the pink sky, a single star in the gathering blue. I thought about how being here might affect my own Swedish identity. I felt ambivalent about going back to London, anticipating missing these late twilight walks. I knew that once I left I would be unlikely to come back, and I was sad about that. My fieldwork was coming to an end. I didn't feel well; a certain shakiness was creeping in, interspersed with a slightly feverish excitement. Many nights were broken, haunted by a recurring sense of the utter strangeness of being there. The days came and went, and I didn't look forward to any of them.

By the beginning of July I had interviewed almost everyone in the village. At that point I went to interview Ivar. He was, unexpectedly, at home, in shorts and a short-sleeved shirt. He looked strong and solid, his feet in old brown socks. I was barefoot. I asked him all the survey questions in Estonian, and then we spoke, both in Estonian and in Swedish. He seemed younger speaking Estonian—we had, up until then, only spoken Swedish. I asked to see the archive of *Samfundet för Estlandssvensk Kultur*, the Society of Estonian Swedish Culture, that he administered, and he jumped up, saying, "One moment! I must tidy up a little." It was a small room with broad metal shelves, stacked with books, about fifteen boxes yet unpacked. In the autumn forty more boxes were coming, a single donation from a Swede he knew. They had also received a grant from the Swedish Institute of about £10,000, a fortune in the context of the village, earmarked for the library.

After Ivar I had only sixteen flats left to survey, people who didn't ever seem to be at home. The traditional Song Festival was on in Tallinn, as was the less well known Dance Festival. I watched some of it on TV, getting up every ten minutes or so to switch the TV off and on when the picture disappeared. At the dance stadium, a horse-drawn carriage with a man and a woman appeared: Kalev and Linda—mythical figures from the Estonian national epic, *Kalevipoeg* ("Kalev's Son"), collated in the nineteenth century from folk tales similar to the Finnish *Kalevala*. The dancers formed themselves into a large cross around them, to a monotonous unaccompanied song. After that each county danced in turn, complex and symbolic dances. West Estonia, Läänemaa, was symbolised by barrels of beer, forming the centre of four circles. On each barrel a man with two beakers in his hands stood, and swayed, with the song. "Beer and the sea," the TV commentator said blandly, "are the two themes from Läänemaa." This was less impressive than the foregoing, but even so something about the aesthetic was appealing: it transcended, and preceded, modern notions of stylishness. The stout figures on the barrels, moving with their beakers, were an image of rural comfort, of Carnival fighting Lent, of strength and fat, of times of plenty.

After that the women started dancing with each other, without the men. They sang, too. An older woman in traditional dress sang the solo part, voice wavering and uneven, all the others around her joining in the chorus. The effect was almost sacral; the significance was in her persona rather than her voice. An eerie chant with drumming followed, and all the dancers formed one large square moving slowly with the music. Linda announced a litany for the dancers: "Dance, dance, our dance." Then she spoke formally, quoting, I think from the *Kalevipoeg*. The men removed their hats. It was very quiet.

My hands swelled from typing too much in the heat. I went for a walk to the abandoned field behind the manor house, beyond the old park, and waded through the tall grass to the tree in the middle. I lay down on the ground, and the wind shook the branches above me. I was hidden from sight. The sun streamed through the green leaves. That evening the scrubby pieces of land between the blocks of flats were turned into hayfields. A boy of about twelve was cutting the long grass with a scythe, two women raking and collecting it behind him. It was the height of summer.

Around that time I went for an all-day cycle ride with Ivar; his friend Allan, the museum director; and Mart Niklus, the MP and former dissident. Niklus was originally a zoologist, specialising in ornithology, who had translated Charles Darwin into Estonian. Antonia Fraser, who was then president of English PEN, wrote about his case in the first 1988 issue of *Index on Censorship*: "The adoption of the Estonian Mart Niklus is in keeping with PEN's policy to support members of 'minority' cultures who believe that their traditions and language have a right to co-exist with those of the great powers." At that time Niklus was serving a ten-year sentence at a "special regime" camp known as Perm 36-1, located in the Permskaya region at the foot of the Ural Mountains. He was due to be released in 1990, followed by five years of internal exile. Because of pressure from PEN, and because of glasnost and perestroika, he was released early, in 1988. Estonian was banned in the camp. Shortly before that article was written he had been beaten for speaking Estonian to his mother, who spoke little Russian, when she visited him. He suffered from radiculitis, a form of spinal nerve inflammation, and stomach pains. He had been on hunger strike many times. "His most recent sentence," Antonia Fraser ended her article, "was for 'anti-Soviet agitation and propaganda.'"

Article 62 of the 1977 Soviet Constitution

1. Citizens of the USSR are obliged to safeguard the interests of the Soviet state, and to enhance its power and prestige.
2. Defence of the Socialist Motherland is the sacred duty of every citizen of the USSR.
3. Betrayal of the Motherland is the gravest of crimes against the people.

We cycled first to Saare. Herbert, a farmer, and his wife drove us on their lorry through newly cut hayfields on to some moorland in the southern part of the peninsula. We left the lorry and walked: Mart Niklus barefoot; Ivar with binoculars and a small round smile; Herbert, tall and intense, smiling, gold tooth glinting; his wife striding along behind him. Essentially we were looking for birds, for Mart Niklus, but we also had a destination: a huge split rock near the sea. The flat quiet land was eerie, like a savannah, with a high sky. At times we had to cut a path through stretches of reed, Mart Niklus walking gingerly, last, toes bleeding.

Herbert and his wife invited us for sandwiches in their garden afterwards: a plate of jam and one of pate, Fanta "for the women," beer for the men, and coffee. Afterwards he drove us back to Pürksi. I sat in happy silence with Ivar and the bikes on the back of the lorry. It was still morning. Now we cycled west to the sea, where I swam, alone, and we ate our picnic. We tried, after that, to take a shortcut through the uninhabited area in the northwest of the peninsula, but we couldn't get through. Instead we followed an overgrown road leading us back the way we came. We cycled on towards the church and Hara, through the scent of the newly cut hay and the flowers.

Niklus identified birds from their song in perfect English, Allan talked about the Soviet curriculum of the history degree in Tartu, and Ivar was quiet, with a pleased and only slightly ironic smile.

Outside Hara by the sea we had our second picnic. "We must eat everything now, you see," Niklus told me. By this time we were tired and giggly, and Ivar started telling jokes. I now remember only the one about the Estonian definition of hell. The answer was a group of Latvians singing around the campfire with their arms around one another: Estonian ironic disdain.

We had already seen one Soviet watchtower where I swam, and now we cycled on towards another. We climbed up the rusty and rickety staircase, and stood in the little chamber of rotting wood at the top. An old sign described, in Russian, what to do if an enemy was sighted at sea. There was such a strange dissonance between the sign, the tower, and the guard hut below, and the coastline itself: idyllic blue sea, the evening sun, a family of swans bobbing on the waves.

"They are teaching their children to fish!" said Ivar, delighted, watching through his binoculars.

"Do swans fish?" Allan asked. None of us knew.

The three of us stood close together in the tower. Ivar watched Niklus down below, walking slowly by the water. "He is looking for birds," he said mildly. "Imagine now," he continued, "if we were soldiers up here and he was an enemy down there. What would we do?"

"How did they communicate with the hut?" I asked, and he said, mock impatiently, "They telephoned, they had telephones here, you can still see the wires," which was absurdly funny because there were no wires left; the soldiers took everything like that with them. All the watchtowers and the buildings next to them had a similar feel: abandoned, either building sites or ruins, unfinished or stripped. It was hard to tell whether they had been abandoned before they were ready, and whether they were looted before or after they were abandoned. Those kinds of buildings always looked new—Soviet new—badly laid white-grey bricks, small squat buildings, sometimes with odd towers sticking up from the roof. This one had a random concrete path leading nowhere—it looked as though someone had started it, and then stopped when the concrete ran out.

Moving about on the peninsula, you were constantly reminded of the Soviet times. It was the background to people's conversations, the keynote people always came back to. We stopped at a farm to ask for water, and found a slightly drunk elderly couple, dressed in rags, probably no more than sixty years old, if that. The man had only two front teeth left. They were lowering the bucket to give us some water from the well when their son drove up in an old orange Lada, Soviet cigarette in his mouth. The daughter-in-law was in a skimpy red bikini, and there were two watchful little girls in the back, dressed in stiff skirts and tucked in hand-me-down jumpers. We drank the yellowish well water, whilst they talked to us about how the "Russians" had destroyed everything. Later, Allan explained to me that when the "locals" talked about the "Russians," they really should talk about the Soviet *system,* but they were not educated enough to be able to distinguish between the two. It was, ironically, a most Soviet addendum, that intelligentsia complaint about the idiocy of the countryside.

On the way to Hara were a couple of restored farmhouses that had been turned into summerhouses. We cycled past one of them, a green sweep of lawn and two Western but Estonian registered cars on the drive. A couple sunning themselves in swimming costumes and sunglasses looked up from their comfortable chairs, their newspapers: a surreal vision from another world.

We got back to the village just past nine, with me in the lead because I was the most tired. Ivar politely hung back, and shouted merrily as I slowly cycled past the speed sign entering the village: "Sigrid! Slow down! It's seventy here!" Later we had dinner at his flat. I brought over a bean stew I had already made, two bottles of beer, and some vodka. Niklus didn't want any vodka: it was too associated with Soviet alienation and decadence for him—everything he was against.

Ivar energetically chopped onion leaves, a substitute for chives, and mixed it with sour cream. Niklus tried to get us to mix the remaining margarine, all melted now, with the beans, a poignant reminder of his time in the camp. We ate the beans with pasta, and without vodka. "Beans," Allan kept saying sleepily, reminded of *Mr. Bean*, which had been running on TV. After dinner he read aloud from an old hagiography of Stalin, for fun. Niklus left soon afterwards, and Ivar brought out my vodka bottle and put it on the table. I did nothing, not realising that he was waiting for me to offer it, and finally, with a small impatient gesture, he said, "Well, can we pour it out?" and I said, "Yes, yes, of course." Allan mixed the vodka with Swedish custard powder, assuring us slightly defensively that it was very good. He kept falling asleep, whilst Ivar played particular pieces of Estonian music from the mid-1980s for me: grave avant-garde ensembles, some based on folk songs, most with no lyrics. One famous one was dedicated to the typewriter, and featured a typewriter as an instrument, subtly antibureaucratic, and hence anti-Soviet. "That was the time for Estonian music," he said. "Now it's all in English, all the same." Then it was profound and Ugric, monotonous and mystical. How did that evening end? I hardly remember. I left with birdsong and Estonian music in my mind, regretful of the vodka, legs so tired. The next day I woke up burnt by the sun, legs aching. I could barely even open my eyes.

A few days earlier I had driven to the old churchyard in Sutlepa with Herbert Stahl, a Swede from one of the islands. He was nineteen when they were evacuated, following the Soviet invasion. "No damn joke, that," he told me, lifting his black sunglasses. He had been back to the island, which was still heavily mined, and applied to get his land back. There was nothing left of any of the houses or buildings, he said. They were razed to the ground by the Red Army. We wandered about and talked, and he kept straying from the subject to tell me other things about his life, like the time when he was clinically dead from accidental electrocution and woke up in hospital: "I was dead, see, and then I woke up in a soft bed, surrounded by people in white, and I thought, Is this heaven?" He was a fridge repairman, and when Estonia became independent he went to Electrolux, the company he worked for, and told them about his accident and asked for money for the trip over. His manager asked how much he needed, and handed over 3,000 Swedish crowns, some £300, in cash, there and then.

He did tell me a few things about life on the island, mostly in the bar later, stray facts of little use to my research. Marriages, he said, were informally arranged, and with only sixty-seven families there was a lot of intermarriage. Girls knitted competitively. In the end he talked only about his present girlfriends in Estonia, all, he said, wild about him. "I never dare to joke to anyone anymore about marriage," he said smugly, "they take it so seriously." He was so rich, in that context, this retired fridge repairman. I reminded him that we had promised to go up to Ivar's, and he bought a bottle of cherry liqueur to give him. Slightly drunk by now, he flirted heavily with me, to Ivar's obvious amusement. Just as I was leaving he telepathically stood up at the same time, so we had to leave together. He hugged me rather forcefully as I offered him a hand in good night.

After Herbert, another Swede turned up in the village: Tor, a libertarian entrepreneur from Åtvidaberg. He was thinking of leaving Sweden for good and settling here, starting a small firm. He was ex-army, small and heavy, with dark blue, almond-shaped eyes. He, also, talked about all the women he'd met, most of them mothers, all of them poor.

I never quite saw that kind of poverty in the village. The same day I met Tor, I went to post a letter. Ülo's mother had taken charge of the post office whilst Eve was on holiday. She was sitting on a chair behind the counter having her hair cut by a friend. Another friend was watching and talking. They interrupted proceedings to sell me a stamp for England.

"It's two-ninety," she said.

"Isn't it four, actually?" I asked hesitantly, knowing the price by heart.

"No! Two-ninety."

I looked at her, then paid 2.90, put the stamp on the envelope, and handed it back to her, hoping for the best. They were poor too, but it was such a peaceful scene. The absence of the state also meant the absence of rules, so the old alcoholics could sit and drink in the shop, without being harrassed. The mayor's mother could stand in, and have her hair cut whilst working. It was so humane.

ELEVEN

Swirls of Dust

In June there was a festival for the Estonian Swedes, organised from Sweden, with many former refugees attending. Everything was delayed, of course—people were rigging up a TV and video in front of the stage, and there was a murmur of voices. Virve, the Finnish guardian of Swedishness, told me, incensed, "Do you know what I heard when I arrived? An English song!" The exhibition, in the narrow room behind the hall, showed the history of the Estonian Swedes, and people were milling about looking at the display. I looked up, and saw Ivar with an elderly Swedish woman. She had just given him a Swedish aspirin and a throat lozenge. I saw him leave her, to discreetly spit out the lozenge, which he didn't like. She saw me, and muttered quickly to her daughter, "Do you have any more of those aspirins?" She, the daughter, fished out a whole packet, and gave it to me. "They are *over the counter*," the mother explained carefully, in Swedish, "not on *prescription*." "Thank you," I said, trying not to sound too Swedish. She nodded and smiled, gripped my hand, and shook out a handful of medicinal chewing gum, a Swedish speciality, from a box as a gift. I knew that chewing gum, and was happy to have it.

Ivar came up to me. "Busy, isn't it?" he said. "We are about to begin." He crossed over to the hall to close the drapes. A young man from Sweden opened them again, dust clouds whirling, and

Ivar looked at me, shrugging ironically. Swedish TV was filming. A technician was testing the mike on the podium, saying, "One, two, three," over and over. I was filming, too, with my little video camera. A man accidentally stumbled over the tripod. A Swedish boy of about nine standing next to me watched the camera shake. He looked at me impassively, and then reached out and kicked the tripod, quite casually. "Stop it!" I said sternly in English.

The choir, dressed in folk costumes, came onto the stage, and sang. A middle-aged Swede, probably the son of one of the refugees, tried to engage them in conversation afterwards. "So, do you speak Swedish? Did you learn some Swedish in school?" he asked cheerfully. The girls giggled, and one of them finally said, quite incorrectly, "No." I overheard another Swede try to engage one of the men from the village in conversation, in Swedish. He smiled tersely in response, shrugged, and said one English word, "Sorry." In the hall, former refugees were meeting again. Some of them were speaking Estonian, not Swedish: "So, how is life in Canada?" "Oh, it's fine, fine." "Is there a lot of work?" "Oh yes." I was standing around, filming, listening casually to the trivial conversations.

After the singing, there was a show of Swedish ethnographic films about the Swedes in Estonia from the 1930s and 1940s. There were two films about the island of Runö, one of them dating from the 1930s, possibly when Gunnar Schantz, the agronomist and missionary, was still there, the other from 1944. Both of them were silent. They were remarkably alike. In the 1930s film the camera panned over scenes from life on the island, with captions like "The Life of the People," "Traditional Games," "Folk Costumes," "The Boats," "This Island Has Been Inhabited by Swedes since Time Immemorial," "One of the Thatched Roofs in the Village Is Being Re-Laid," "The Harvest of the Hay," "The Harvest of the Rye," "When the Wind Is Suitable the Mills in the Village Grind the Seed," "No One Neglects the Sunday Service," and "Sunday Evenings There Is Almost Always Dancing and Games."

The 1944 film followed. "A Visit to the Swedish Descendants on Runö," read the first caption. "Fishing Huts from the Beach, Several Hundred Years Old," "The Population Is of Ancient Swedish Stock," "Customs and Traditions Are Exceedingly Old-Fashioned," "The Men Are Stately," "The Inhabitants of Runö, Gathered Around the Swedish Flag, Which They Hold in Great Esteem," and, archly, "The So-Called Harbour," and "Butter Churn, Patent Runö."

This 1944 film culminated in the evacuation of Runö, organised and carried out by the Nazis. Smiling SS officers mingled with representatives from the Red Cross. Families surrounded by bundles and boxes gathered on the sandy beach. The Estonian ship *Juhan* was adorned with a swastika. The film cut to the arrival in Sweden. Some people were carried off to waiting ambulances. The camera focused on a smiling blond child in a headscarf, a little knitted purse tied to her wrist. A woman behind me whispered to someone, maybe her sister: "Mummy's knitted bag, do you see, hanging from the wrist? She had one of those." And thus the moment of the SS evacuation passed almost imperceptibly. The film did not comment on it, and neither did the people around me.

I thought of the famous quote from Giuseppe Tomasi di Lampedusa's novel *The Leopard*: "*Se vogliamo che tutto rimanga com'è, bisogna che tutto cambi* [If we want everything to stay the same, everything needs to change]." The two films were so alike that it seemed as though time had stood still. But in fact everything had changed. In the decade or so between them, Estonia had endured war and occupations so brutal that almost one-quarter of the population had disappeared. Thousands of people had been arrested and deported in the first Soviet occupation of 1940–41. Many others had been killed or incarcerated by the Nazis. Tens of thousands of young men had been conscripted by the Red Army and the Wehrmacht. Virtually all the Jews in Estonia had been murdered, and thousands of other people of Jewish origin had been brought to Estonia to be killed. By the time this film was recorded, all the Estonian Jews who had stayed in Estonia except *twelve people*, who had remained hidden, were dead. In the middle of this unprecedented human catastrophe, Swedish filmmakers were writing captions like "The So-Called Harbour" and "Butter Churn, Patent Runö." It was incomprehensible. It was as though the history of the Estonian Swedes took place in a parallel universe.

Earlier, in Stockholm, I had interviewed a man from Runö, the writer Jakob Steffensson. "Everybody was equal there," he said. "It was an authentically communist society. Nothing was paid for with money, and all the work was collective." They fished and farmed and hunted seal. They sold seal blubber and skins, and smoked and ate the seal meat, except, he said, the old bulls, which were too salty. Steffensson had no memory or knowledge of Schantz, was barely born when he left the island, and had no conception of his modernising measures, or how much development had taken place through his activities. He did, however, remember the Soviet and Nazi occupations.

"We danced with the Russians and we danced with the Germans," he said. Runö had its own SS officer, *Oberleutnant* Lienhardt. Steffenson took him shooting and seal hunting. Lienhardt, he said, had wanted to organise independence for the Runö people and be their führer. He also tried, unsuccessfully, to persuade people to come to Germany to train as Nazi local administrators. Why didn't they go? Most people, Steffenson said, didn't believe the Germans would win the war, despite their claims in 1944 that in another six weeks Leningrad would fall.

So there it was. Lienhardt's colleagues were running the Estonian concentration camps on the mainland whilst he was hunting seals on Runö. The two histories never touch one another: people writing about the camps never mention the Swedes, and vice versa. But they were only a few miles apart.

Lienhardt organised the final evacuation of the islanders to Sweden, and other SS officers did the same for the other Swedish communities. The Swedish state paid them 50 Swedish crowns, about £5, per person. On Runö, all but 6 of the 350 or so inhabitants fled to Sweden. Lists were made of the size of their farms and their belongings. Some believed, on the basis of those lists, that they would get compensation in Sweden for the farms they had abandoned, but they never did. They were also told, by the authorities who received them in Sweden, to keep quiet about the evacuation.

Steffensson took part in an early 1990s Swedish documentary entitled *Back to Runö*. He gave me a video of it. Several old people, dressed in their folk costumes, stepped out of a helicopter, knelt down, and kissed the ground. One of the women who had stayed on the island was interviewed. Her husband had been deported soon after the exodus of the islanders, and she had temporarily moved to the mainland. When they eventually came back many years later, all the hazel and all the apple trees had been cut down. The island was resettled after the Swedes left, first by Russians, probably refugees—*drifters*, she said—who moved into the empty houses. Eventually they left, I don't know why or where. Estonians from other islands started to take over the houses, one by one. By 1990 they were still there, alongside a handful of remaining Soviet troops.

Steffensson visits his old family farm, Isaksgården. "What a disaster," he says, "everything is ruined, everything, everything. I am just, I am not upset, I can't find words. It is so immensely sad. Now I pass away."

And it was sad. The harbour was rebuilt in shabby concrete, and the local culture seemed hopeless and alcoholic.

As for Lienhardt, he bought a manor house in Sweden, was extradited to Germany after the war, and fled to South America. Eventually he made his way back to Germany. Steffensson went to see him there, he told me, in some small town, I can't remember which. He was a bitter old man by then, living alone in a small flat. His dream, he told Steffensson, was to have become the lighthouse keeper of Runö.

* * *

I don't think the Estonian Swedes, on the whole, were Nazi sympathisers. They were a minority, and their journals and cultural activism played a small part in the vibrant 1930s debate about minority rights in Europe. The Nazis, with their demented dreams of ethnic German supremacy, had no time for minorities: their worldview was based on the idea of majority power, of might is right. Articles in the Estonian Swedish journals often made explicit reference to the debate about the rights of minorities. The Swedes were a minority within another minority, the Estonians, stacked like Russian dolls, trapped between Russia and Germany. The Estonian Swedish debate mirrored the Estonian debate, which mirrored debates all over Europe. The Swedes were on the liberal side, therefore. But whether they approved of the Nazis or not, it is true that the Nazis approved of them. Approved of them enough, anyway, to accept a deal to evacuate them to Sweden, for a payment, to peace and neutrality. But the evacuation came at a price: the Nazis destroyed the reputations of their few favoured minorities. Everything they liked became suspect after the war: cornfields and blond children, women in folk costumes gathering hay, blond plaits swinging, soldiers marching in formation. Only the countries behind the iron curtain could—and did—promote those kinds of images after the end of the war. They were culturally immune to the Nazi taint. Indeed, as part of the effort to undermine and destroy "bourgeois nationalism," the communists promoted their own brand of "folk nationalism," an endless stream of folky kitsch—national festivals, traditional dress, folk dancing—almost indistinguishable from Nazi propaganda.

The war ended Swedishness in Estonia. Between the two World Wars the minority Swedes had been much written about in Sweden, often in highly sentimental terms. They had been visited, helped, photographed, interviewed, and filmed. Their primitive farmhouses, their poverty, and their quiet struggle to preserve their ethnic identity had been moving, then. People had wanted to help them. But after the war, everything changed. In Sweden there was shame about the perhaps overly collaborative neutrality. Iron ore, essential for the Nazi war effort, was sold and transported to Germany from the Swedish mines in the north, whilst German troops were transported north through Sweden to aid the Finnish army fighting the Red Army. Many Swedes were sympathetic to that battle: "Finland's cause is ours!" ran the slogan. There was shame about the many Nazi sympathisers in parliament, in the universities, and in the press. There was shame about the restrictions on Jewish immigration before the war, when the writing was so clear on the wall.

The context was shifting. The story of the Estonian Swedes was becoming parochial. So many others, who had also made their way to Sweden, had suffered so much more than they had. Some fifteen thousand Jewish survivors were rescued from the concentration camps by Folke Bernadotte, Count of Wisborg and the Swedish Red Cross, in their rescue mission at the end of the war, and taken to Sweden to recover. There were other refugees, too: some seventy thousand Finnish children had been evacuated during the war. Many Swedish families, including mine, took responsibility for a Finnish "war child." Most of the Jews in Denmark, more than seven thousand people, were secretly evacuated across the sound to Sweden before their final deportation to concentration camps, in October 1943. The German attaché Georg Ferdinand Duckwitz had leaked the deportation plan to Danish Social Democrat Hans Hedtoft, who in turn had contacted the Jewish community leaders. The underground, aided by sympathetic locals on both sides of the sound, carried out the evacuation.

In Europe there were displaced people everywhere, probably about eleven million people all in all. By the end of 1945 some six million European refugees, Jews and eastern Europeans fleeing communism, had been repatriated by the Allied forces and the

United Nations Relief and Rehabilitation Authority (UNRRA, founded in 1943, when the term "United Nations" still referred to the Allied forces). There were, also, millions of ethnic German refugees, who were not part of the UNRRA remit. By 1947 relative order had been restored, but there were still some 850,000 traumatised and dispossessed people left in the limbo of displaced persons (DP) camps in Europe. The last DP camp, Föhrenwald, a former slave labour camp attached to the IG Farben workforce in Bavaria, closed in 1957. It was run by Henry Cohen from New York, whose parents had emigrated from Vilna in Lithuania. He had fought in the infantry, and was only twenty-three years old when he was assigned responsibility for *Föhrenwald* and its fifty-six hundred Jewish inmates. He did it well, it seems, working with a camp committee; seeing to sanitation and supplies; setting up schools; and encouraging Zionism, youth movements, vocational training, religious activities, music, theatre, and a weekly newspaper, while also bringing attention to anti-Semitism in the American armed forces. But that's another story. The point is this: in the context of the Holocaust and the war, in the context of millions of displaced people, the evacuation of the Estonian Swedes eventually didn't seem like a big story, even in Sweden. The world was becoming more international. The cold war, and the proxy wars, began, and came to dominate the second half of the twentieth century.

There was silence about the Swedes in Estonia, too, after the war. People with relatives abroad—and there was not a single Swede left in Estonia without relatives abroad—were generally suspect in the Soviet Union. Most of the few remaining Swedes assimilated quietly. Any family history other than of the most proletarian kind could be dangerous, and most people didn't talk about the past, or challenge what their children learnt in the Soviet history lessons in the schools. It was not safe. History, in the sense of a shared national narrative, a dynamic and evolving conversation, was lost to ideology and political repression. And many, perhaps most, of the people conducting that cultural conversation—historians, journalists, writers, archivists, museum curators, reporters, teachers, editors, publishers, documentary filmmakers and producers, and many others—were gone: they had fled, or been deported, or killed.

Weeks after I left Estonia, in September 1994, the Stockholm-bound ferry *Estonia* was shipwrecked in a storm. More than eight hundred people drowned—the precise figure was never known because the Tallinn ticket office didn't keep proper records. I had arrived on that ship, and left on it, too. It was garish and cheerful, ordinary to the Swedes, luxurious to the Estonians.

The long heatwave of the summer had broken, and the night of the disaster was stormy. Water somehow got into the hold, and started slushing around, exaggerating the movement from the waves, rocking the ship from side to side, until it finally tipped over. Many people were trapped in their cabins, or in the public rooms. Others had prepared themselves, gathering on deck in life vests. There were lifeboats, but not enough. Some people fought, in panic, to get into them, others helped each other. Hypothermia in the cold water was lethal, and people struggled to keep each other awake. It was hours before the first helicopters arrived from Finland, the ferry long since disappeared, sinking like a stone, hundreds of meters, to the bottom of the deep sea. Timo was on the *Estonia* the night of the disaster, and survived. The new Swedish teacher, Katarina's replacement, was too. She did not survive.

Years later, I watched a Swedish documentary about the disaster. I wrote about this in my academic book, and I am repeating it here. The Swedish survivors had obviously told their story many times before: they were fluent, confident, even dramatic. The Estonian survivors, by contrast, were hesitant and awkward. There were long silences and stumbling sentences. The Swedes had probably had trauma counselling, helping them to form their experiences into narratives. The Estonians, on the other hand, seemed never to have told anyone what happened to them on that night. Even allowing for different reactions to the TV cameras in their living rooms, and a less empowered relationship with the outside world, it was still as if the very culture of routinely creating stories from memories had been ruptured. The memories remained fragmented; an incoherent flotsam of odd details.

Watching it I was reminded of George Orwell's *1984*. Winston, asking some "proles" in a pub whether life was better or worse before the revolution, couldn't get a coherent answer: "They remembered a million useless things, a quarrel with a work-mate, a hunt for a lost bicycle pump, the expression on a long-dead sister's face, the swirls of dust on a windy morning seventy years ago: but all the relevant facts were outside the range of their vision." The memories of the older people I met on the peninsula were similarly fragile and incoherent. We underestimate, I think, how much our individual stories are supported by a mutual understanding of shared history. We refer to the *zeitgeist* of the decades in coded shorthand. Each decade eventually gains a dominant symbolic narrative—think of the 1920s, or the 1960s—within which our individual memories and stories are contextualised. In the West there is an easy relationship between individual lives and national culture and history. If that relationship, however, becomes fraught with danger, if that scaffolding of history and culture, and all the countless and various investigations into it, which is one of the defining activities of liberal democracies, ceases to exist, then your understanding of who you are in the world, who your family is, and what your town and country is, becomes fragmented. The stories (the history) of the people I met were not shored up by official and public versions of events, nor told sufficiently often to have created fluency and certainty. They just about knew what had happened, but they had no proper context for the story yet. Like Winston's "proles," they couldn't give coherent answers.

Winston, on his own, couldn't make sense of the information contained in the seemingly inconsequential answers he got. But

those answers were exactly the kind of odd details Orwell himself collected in *Down and Out in Paris and London, The Road to
Wigan Pier*, and other works. One of the political points made by
the book, then, must be this: that Winston couldn't do what his
creator Orwell had done—create meaning and narrative from odd
details—not just because the gap between him and the "proles"
had become too wide, but also because the system of Ingsoc had
destroyed the framework of social history and journalism needed
to organise fragments into narrative. Narratives are not just about
accumulations of facts; the theoretical frameworks are essential for
creating stories. The people on the collective farm had no framework
for their stories, now that the Soviet version of history, which no
one had much believed in anyway, had become discredited. The past
was always vague and anecdotal: The soldiers came knocking on
doors. People disappeared. You never heard from them. Decades
later some came back. Others didn't.

Swedes were not allowed to fish or join fishing collective farms
after the invasion. Two young men, I heard, had tried to escape by
boat to Sweden in the 1960s. They built the boat in secret. It took a
long time, and it wasn't a very good boat. They were caught, on the
sea. One of them died in prison. No one I spoke to knew what he
had died of, or the details of what happened, or even their names.
Just like it was taken for granted that houses could be abandoned
and slowly decay, so it was taken for granted that people died in
prisons, and that it was possible that no one would really ever know
the cause of death. That is the nature of totalitarianism.

Now the era of lost history is over. On the peninsula, Ivar,
Allan, the Estonian Swedish activist Ain Sarv, and many others were
patiently researching and teaching history. When I was there, this
process was just beginning; now much of the historical research is
easily available online, in English as well as Estonian. In the early
1990s no one knew numbers, or dates, or statistics—the archives
were just beginning to open. People didn't even have proper maps,

and Soviet repression still lingered in prisons and orphanages, despite occasional scandals revealed by investigating journalists or charities.

On the collective farm it wasn't just that history was lost. Contemporary events, too, were not discussed, and soon forgotten. After my arrival on the collective farm, in September 1993, the greatest constitutional crisis Russia had faced since the 1918 revolution unravelled. The political scene in Russia had become increasingly polarised between supporters of Boris Yeltsin's extreme austerity reforms and critics of those reforms. Aleksandr Rutskoy, Yeltsin's deputy, and Ruslan Khasbulatov, Yeltsin's former ally in the 1991 coup, emerged as the leaders of the anti-Yeltsin protests. On 1 September Yeltsin tried, unsuccessfully, to suspend Rutskoy, accusing him publicly of "corruption." Later that month he wanted to appoint the liberal Yegor Gaidar deputy prime minister and deputy premier for economic affairs, and again he failed. On 21 September 1993 Yeltsin tried to dissolve the Congress of People's Deputies and the Supreme Soviet, which had turned against him, and where criticisms of the economic austerity programme had escalated dangerously. The deputies retaliated with an impeachment, and appointed Rutskoy acting president. There was a standoff, which ended when the army, after some deliberation, and with dubious legality, took Yeltsin's side. On 4 October it stormed the White House, the building of the Supreme Soviet, and arrested Rutskoy and Khasbulatov. Fights broke out in the streets, but were quickly suppressed. Government sources claim that 187 people were killed. The real number may have been higher—Yeltsin's critics put them closer to 2,000. Yeltsin won, though it was a bloody victory. The critics of extreme austerity, some communist and some nationalist, lost, and the power of the presidency grew, paving the way for Vladimir Putin's authoritarian government.

I watched the news with Toivo and Inna. The Russian channel broadcast scenes of mayhem on the streets of Moscow. Khasbulatov and Rutskoy had been arrested, and the news anchor stated that about twenty people had been killed, and some thirty wounded. Neither Inna nor Toivo commented as we looked blankly at the scenes unfolding. My diary records that we had soup for dinner that night, and bread with tinned pork, and that we ate almost in silence. It was dark outside and silent inside, one state reflecting the other. The kettle was howling like the wind. A dog barked, answered by another one far away. Inna, later, made me a cup of tea. Erki, their son, knocked on my door, and said in his hoarse teenage voice, "Sigrid. I have apple."

In Tallinn, by contrast, Veevi sat up with her friends listening to the radio all night, and talked of nothing else. A few days earlier a bomb had exploded at the American embassy in Tallinn, which they thought was certainly connected with the events, orchestrated by a well-organised network of provocateurs. In Veevi's view, Yeltsin had done battle with the communists and won; she was relieved and triumphant. On the collective farm, such current affairs passed us by. Even developments of local significance were largely ignored. I am thinking once again about the day the sign for the Noarootsi Kolhoos on the culture hall was taken down, and replaced by a new gleaming sign for a commercial bank. It might have been a momentous event: the proper end of the collective farm. But no one commented, and no one, seemingly, cared. This was at least six months after the members of the collective farm had formally voted it out of existence, but the sign had remained in place. The bank branch, incidentally, never did open, and that sign, too, was eventually removed.

People on the collective farm knew almost nothing about the Nazi occupation, or the Holocaust, and they knew very little about the Stalinist occupation. For most people on the peninsula, even local history, and the small lost civilisation of the Estonian Swedes had been only a vague rumour in the 1960s and 1970s. Though they were now becoming aware of the current aid programme and revival, no one, except Ivar, really knew much about it. One of my students wrote the following beguiling essay about the Estonian Swedes:

> I believe that minorities in Estonia is many. But I tell to you of this nationality what threatens die out and where I actually belong. And so! I talk Coastswedens. My grandmother is Coastswede and in she's talk and my own the study ground try I do this work . . . Coastswedens have our language. They have our customs. They's language resemble the Swedish language. Here village where I live was before 27 homestead with 250 peoples. Now is here only 6 homestead with 17 peoples from theirs only one coastsweden— my grandmother. Swedes was living very well. Swedens have here a pot of schools. In this village school was from village 3 km. School building was grand estate. That is now remain. In the school was only sex classes. When swedes are want forward learn have to they command the Estonian language. Estonian and swedes get through well. Swedes is fighting a long time our from freedom before. That was so 1920/30. Then came war. Many Swedes flee in Swerige. Few peoples come back. The Soviet system not tolerate aliens. Coastswedes sustain a loss. Now strive I, that I get in passport Swede.

The people on the peninsula didn't know about the successive waves of the Swedish cultural revival before the war, the cultural debates in the Swedish newspapers and journals, the Swedish schools, the 1930s activism for minority rights, and the energetic and innovative development efforts. Even so, despite the historical amnesia, the culture of the Estonian Swedes was being revived again, for the third time in a hundred years, using very much the same methods, the same cheerful discourse—"help to self-help!"—and the same ideas. It wasn't just the culture of the Estonian Swedes that was

revived in the 1990s: the tradition of revival itself was being reinvented, that particular combination of cultural advocacy and local
development initiatives that was so effective, then as now.

In 1984 the Swedish communist Sven Bjelf published a
staunchly pro-communist book (in Moscow) about the Swedes in
the Soviet Union. Most of the people he wrote about were Swedish
communists from the mining areas in the north, who had emigrated
to the Soviet Union in the 1920s and 1930s. The people he met
were, he claimed, still staunchly supportive of the Soviet system:
"Imagine," one of them says, "it's fifty years since I arrived in the
Soviet Union. So much has changed and improved in those years.
The country is completely transformed. I and all Soviet citizens
have a good life now. We are actually spoilt, so spoilt that we forget
how good life is. Who really thinks about the obvious things, such
as rent, which is as cheap now as it was fifty years ago. Who thinks
about the fact that visits to the doctor are free, and that medicine
is so cheap, just a few kopek. At least us pensioners, I am not sure
about younger people, get new teeth for free. All studies, whatever
they are, are free, with scholarships. Communications are cheap.
There is so much one doesn't notice because it's become a habit
that everything should be cheap or free."

The teeth are a telling point: the communists who emigrated
were not to know that in Sweden old people, on the whole, still
had their own teeth: diet and dental care had seen to that. Bjelf
also wrote about Gammalsvenskby, a Swedish village in Ukraine. In
1781 about a thousand Swedes from the Estonian island of Dagö
had a dispute with their feudal landowner, Magnus Stenbock, about
their right not to become serfs. Catherine the Great intervened,
and gave the Swedes formerly Ottoman land in Ukraine, which
she wanted to resettle with her own people. They had little choice
but to go, and set off on a long and arduous journey south. At least
half the Dagö Swedes died on the way, and many more died on

arrival. The survivors, however, established a village, and called it Gammalsvenskby ("Old Swedish Village"), where, improbably, some of their descendants still live, and still speak Swedish.

In 1929 the inhabitants of the village, after years of petition-ing, were given permission to return to Sweden. There, faced with depression and unemployment, a few of them, encouraged by the Swedish Communist Party, decided to return to Ukraine. They got a hero's welcome there, and much publicity, but quite soon the repres-sion and hunger, the political violence, and the orchestrated famine that killed millions of people trapped in dying villages, devastated the community. About twenty of the villagers were arrested after yet another petition to move back to Sweden, and some were sent to prison. Stalinist purges later led to more arrests, and some executions.

Most of the remaining Swedes from the village were evacuated by the Nazis along with German-speaking civilians in the retreat of 1943. They ended up in Poland, where they were again caught up in Stalinist repression, the majority deported to the Gulag. Soon after the war, however, Poland negotiated to give land to the Soviet Union in return for the release of Polish prisoners in the Gulag. The Swedes, too, were handed over in that deal. The survivors made their way back to the Swedish village by 1947. It was, by then, a broken community.

Bjelf went there when he was researching his fawning book, and was introduced to the model worker and Swedish descendant Igor Annas: "As we meet and shake hands in the yard I see that Igor Annas has very clear blue eyes. In contrast to so many of us in Sweden he looks like a real Swedish Viking. His grip makes it clear what a powerful man he is." A photograph shows Annas's handsome head and shoulders from below, with a Soviet harvester behind him, smiling, hair combed back, in the iconic stance of a Stakhanovite worker-hero.

I visited Gammalsvenskby in 1996. The village is on the Dnieper River, on the fertile Ukrainian plain. It is no more than a few streets of small huddled houses, electrical wires hanging slackly between uncertain poles, along with a handful of modern buildings. I was given sweet tea and meat salad and biscuits in the culture hall, before being taken to visit some old people who still spoke Swedish. They had spent part of their childhood in Sweden before travelling back with their parents to the black and fertile soil of Ukraine, to what turned out to be hunger and violence, to the very epicentre of Stalinist and Nazi violence.

I remember the river and the mud. I remember Odessa, where the immigration officer tried to steal my husband's passport by passing back a closed and empty leather cover. I remember the look that passed like a current between the armed guards in the room when he went back to reclaim it. I remember the flat land, the long drive, the black fields and the broad river. But I have no real sense of the history of the village. My conversation with the old Swedes was as fragmented as the conversations I had on the collective farm. There was just one unexpected thing: one old woman said that when the villagers left for Sweden they "sold the village to Jews." I hadn't heard that before, so I asked what happened. There was a Jewish village nearby, she said. They moved in. Then the war started. The Jews disappeared. She looked down at the table—that was it. And this was where, finally, all the histories met: the parallel histories of the Estonian Swedes, the war, the Gulag, the repression, the hunger, and the Holocaust. She didn't say much about it. At the very centre of the story of living without history there were only a few words, then silence.

Recently I found a reference to this history online, in a paper about the Swedes from Gammalsvenskby who had emigrated to Canada, in a Canadian academic journal dated 2005. It is one incidental sentence: "Meanwhile Jews from neighboring colonies had taken over the houses vacated by the emigrants." It's clear from the context that Swedes leaving Ukraine had put up their houses for sale, and that Jewish neighbours had in fact bought them. "Taken over" is, I think, perhaps slightly misleading, in this context. But at least the history is written.

Twelve

Summer

In Pürksi, the Swedish festival carried on. After most of the visitors had gone back to the holiday village on the mainland to rest before the evening party, the villagers came in to look at the part of it dedicated to Soviet life, situated in a remote corner. Ivar showed it to me, laughing his particular ironic laugh. There were photographs of harvesters and tractors, of model workers, of celebrations of International Women's Day, of processions and folk dancing. People quietly looked at the photographs and Russian slogans, leafed through the collective farm records, the Russian and Soviet Estonian books, and the school photograph albums. It was their recent past, now more in danger of being forgotten than the history of the minority Swedes.

In the evening Werner, the manager of Gorbyland, once again transformed himself into a rock singer with a synthesiser. He sang hoarse Estonian rock in that dark and chilly hall with a flickering candle on the piano. Few of the Swedes staying in the holiday village, in fact, had come back from their rest. Some young people were dancing together, but the hall was almost empty. A few children ran from corner to corner, and Virve sat on a chair, looking on with her characteristic mixture of humour, resignation, and superiority.

The next day there was a Swedish memorial service in the church, preceded by a procession of returning refugees. A vicar from Stockholm prayed with them, the best known of all Swedish prayers, the rhyming children's prayer "God Who Holds All Children Dear." "You all know this one," he said cosily. The prayer set the tone, followed by hymns and songs echoing with a nostalgic evocation of Swedishness. The vicar was, I learnt, the son-in-law of Dannel, the Swedish vicar on the peninsula who had fled after the Soviet invasion. He ended the service with a bland midsummer prayer. I remembered, in contrast, the furious, powerful midsummer fire in the night, whipped by the storm and the rain.

Outside, by the war monument, I happened to stand next to two rebellious Swedes. "Are we going to stand here for two hours now?" one of them said mutinously, in a low voice, to the other. Two women in traditional dress were arranged by the vicar as posterns. The extended family of the two next to me were told to gather together for one more picture. The other man said impatiently to his friend, "Gathering together, gathering together, gathering together." The vicar, undaunted, began to sing "Who Can Sail without the Wind?," the Christian love song. Despite concerted efforts by the organisers, at least a third of the people refused to collect by the monument, drifting through the surrounding cemetery instead, looking at the gravestones. "Is there a village song we can sing now?" the vicar said innocently. He didn't understand that there were no village songs left. The songs that people still remembered after the war had been taken over by the Soviet authorities in their attempts to make the folk culture Soviet, and later by the dissidents to help turn Estonia back into a country. Those songs no longer had anything to do with ordinary people in an impoverished village in a former border protection zone, people longing for the next episode of *Rosa Salvaje*, the Mexican TV show. No one volunteered, and the moment petered out.

*   *   *

By mid-July I had finished my survey. Time was passing, and I was longing to leave. The daydreams about staying were gone now. I spent most of my time working in Ivar's library, for the historical part of my thesis. Some men outside were digging channels for new telephone cables—already the village was changing. One day there was a sporting event, a remnant from the collective farm time when all the Estonian farms named Lenin met to compete every year. I was ill, not much, but in-between ill, so that I didn't know if it was psychosomatic or not—my useless fever scanner lighted up at 37 and 38 degrees centigrade and ended uncertainly on 38, my coffee tasted of nothing, my right eye was swollen as if I hadn't slept, and I was enormously tired, leaden. It was a beautiful morning, though, of white-blue sky. The lace curtain billowed into my room, and I heard children's voices mingling with a dog barking and a car starting. Eventually I walked out to look at the games. It was very hot. People walked around in tiny bikinis and shorts, drinking beer and playing volleyball. A music system rigged up to a van played loud music, old Swedish hits to start with, later Estonian pop music. People were having fun, much more fun than they had with the returning Swedes. The Swedish question was ignored for the day, and the village went back to what it might have been before, drenched in heat, in beer and volleyball, children left to their own devices. It was a different world.

In late July I went to film Ruth. She was dressed up, and read, dramatically, from her latest notebook, standing on the steps of her cottage. It was very windy, and the sun was glaring, so after a while I suggested that we go inside. For the first time she took me up to the first floor of her cottage. There were two small rooms there, with old iron bedsteads, some old tools, and old postcards covering the yellowing wallpaper on the bulging walls. This was her museum to the Ölvingssons, the Swedish missionary family, who escaped in 1944—a museum no one ever saw, where no one ever went, but a museum nevertheless. She told me how Maria Ölvingsson, née Sedman, had hidden her husband in a hole in the ground, under an unhinged old door covered with earth, and even a small tree. She would sing him warnings in Swedish as the Russian soldiers came looking for him. He evaded deportation, and they escaped.

That same night I went for a walk at sunset, slowly, past the storks picking on the fields, a sparrow hawk chasing a small bird. It threw itself backwards and forwards so quickly that the hawk missed it, and suddenly veered away, flying low over the fields. I walked back on the road, passed by little Ladas and Skodas, families. The men waved, the women stared straight ahead. A Mitsubishi from Finland, a rare sight, passed me, and the driver waved, thinking me a local, I supposed. It was high summer. I didn't have much time left.

At the end of July Virve was going back to Helsinki. The heatwave had lasted for weeks already, and I invited her over for a last cold drink before she left. She sat at my kitchen table drinking peach juice, looking at me with her inscrutable brown eyes. This had been her last year on the collective farm. After several years of teaching there, she was going back to Finland for good.

Later I went over to the Swedish charity sale in the culture hall. There were lots of cars outside, and a queue of maybe seventy people when I came, mostly from the village, but a few I didn't recognise, who had come in from the mainland. I joined the queue, but some of my friends ushered me ahead. "Here comes the press!" they shouted, laughing, insisting I go straight in. The Swedish organisers only let in about ten people at a time, every twenty minutes or so. I wandered about amongst the fridges and piles of shoes and T-shirts and baby clothes. The customers walked around in silence, looking at it all.

Earlier I had spent several hours working in Ivar's library. He had made new potatoes and tomato and onion salad with sour cream, with tinned fatty pork, for me, talking with enthusiasm about a popularity diagram he had drawn for his class. He showed me the diagram, showing who was most and least popular in his class. He was planning to show it to them as an example of Western "sociological method." The lines were colour coded and simple to understand. One girl had not a single line showing that other people liked her drawn to her name, and it seemed not to occur to Ivar that this was problematic. The tools for understanding society were coming back, but it was a piecemeal process, untempered, as yet, by social criticism.

That evening Tor, the Swedish entrepreneur, came to pick me up for a *shashlik* at the bar by the harbour. "Everybody who speaks Swedish is there," he said cosily, "so I was sent to fetch you." I drank too many vodka tonics on that mosquito-ridden evening, watching the dancing, sitting mainly with Marika, the vet. At about three in the morning Marika drove us all home, unsteadily. As soon as we arrived I realised I had left my bag behind, and we drove back, all of us, through the white night, on the small road meandering through the fields, listening to the first birds. We had Sprite and coffee before finally walking home. The stars were fading by then, and the scent of the hay drifted up with the mist on the fields.

In July I visited Narva, the largest city of east Estonia, with Tor. Narva was then almost entirely Russian, and we were to meet a Russian couple who wanted to start a Swedish society there. We arrived in the early evening, driving past old people chatting on comfortable benches outside postwar apartment buildings. The streets were wide and empty. We found our modest hotel, and, armed with only an address, set off to find the Russians. They, Vladik and Marika, were not at home, so we had dinner in a restaurant instead. A cat lazily stretched out on the carpet, and a mangy dog trotted past a few times. There was an orchestra of grey-faced old men, and an elderly waitress with bleached hair. We ate meat salad, and a dry piece of meat with potatoes, and drank tea with sugar melting in the bottom of the glass. We moved twice to avoid the orchestra, the musicians shrugging at me regretfully.

After dinner we returned to the house of the Russians, and this time Vladik, who turned out to be Georgian, opened the door. We waited with his seven-year-old daughter whilst he left to get Marika, his Russian wife. The girl bravely did her best to entertain us, showing us her toys, teaching Tor Russian words, and switching the channels on the old television. After nearly forty minutes her parents returned, and moved immediately into the kitchen to prepare dinner. They stayed there, again, for nearly forty minutes, whilst their daughter continued staunchly to entertain us. It was like being in an experimental film from the 1960s, where the waiting is the substance, and the point. Finally they brought out a festive meal: sausages and mashed potatoes, salads and pickles, a small plate of raspberries and another plate of yogurt and Western chocolates, red lemonade and the Swedish bottle of Absolut vodka that Tor had brought as a present.

We talked about the Swedish friendship organisation they had started, in German, which Vladik barely spoke, Marika and I mixed with Estonian, and Tor spoke passably. They had read a lot about the Swedish connection in the newspapers, they said. They already had fifty-eight members. The key member, they said, was a Swede called Blomfelt, born in 1907, whose parents had immigrated to Russia at the time of the revolution, and who now lived in Narva. Blomfelt was, they confessed when we pressed the point, the only Swedish member. We couldn't meet him, because he was in St. Petersburg. By the end, after a political discussion, where they maintained that the laws were bad, especially the Estonian language requirements for citizenship, but that they loved all people—Estonians, too—whilst Tor stubbornly, and slightly tipsily, maintained that the situation was "not only a problem but also an opportunity," they suddenly asked, intently, if it was possible for them to buy a washing machine in Sweden for dollars.

The next day they took us to the great Kreenholm textile factory. In its heyday it had had twelve thousand employees. Now three thousand people worked there. Tor, an opportunistic entrepreneur, wanted to order fabric. We were taken to a boardroom, where a sceptical blond young man received us. Tor discussed the order, somewhat tensely—he had left his business cards in the car, he claimed—whilst Vladik and Marika rang various numbers from the telephone in a corner of the room. We continued to a furniture factory, where he confidently ordered a thousand drawers. I sank into a chair, still weak from the night before.

After lunch we drove to the beach to rest. I wanted to swim, but Vladik told me that the water was dangerous, toxic with algae blooms. "She is used to it," he said, nodding to his young daughter, who was splashing and frolicking in the water. Tor was stretched out on the sand like a sea lion next to Marika, to whom he had taken a liking. I didn't swim, and contemplated instead what fates had taken me to this place, to Tor, and to this couple who were faking a Swedish connection to create a slightly wider stage for themselves in the narrow niche of post-Soviet capitalism. Tor was a libertarian, and knew, of course, that they weren't Swedish, but liked them all the better for it.

Tor had kept bees in Sweden. On the way home from Narva he told me about sitting between two beehives, taking pollen notes, checking the colour of the pollen against a chart, and occasionally catching an irritated and swollen bee to examine it. The sun was shining, the bees were humming, and he felt absolutely at peace. As he told the story, we were approaching Kunda, the old cement factory town. I think at that point the old factory might still have been working—just. The streets, cars, and houses were covered in white cement dust, like snow. We got out of the car to get a better look. It was an ecological disaster: silent, empty, and tragic. No bees could survive there.

In early August the grey geese came back from the north. The storks had already left. One evening I walked all the way to Paslepa manor, the former Russian base; a strange, humid evening, with a grey haze over the sun and fields, and clouds of silent mosquitos attacking my legs. The whole summer I had been plagued by the flies on the collective farm. I had arrived too late in the season the previous year to have seen much of them, other than the dead flies in the corridor of the "hotel." By May they were back, numerous, fearless and aggressive. They flew straight into your face to get at the eyes. I had never seen European flies behave like that—our flies, I now think, must be weakened by insecticides, and starved by efficient sanitation and rubbish disposal.

That same day I had happened to be at the shop when the food deliveries arrived in the middle of the morning. Five women—customers—were waiting, whilst the supplies were carried in by a couple helped by two small children: crates of beer, lemonade, bread, sausage, boxes of things. We waited together for forty-five minutes whilst the shopkeeper meticulously rearranged all the goods. A large woman in front of me was running her fingers through the hair of her ten-year-old boy; there was no sense of impatience. Later a few young strangers with name badges sauntered through the village, probably here on the Swedish language course. They seemed rather glamorous. I found myself, to my shame, staring at them like a local.

That evening I found Marika and Alar and Heli drinking cock-tails: 96 percent ethanol from Marika's veterinary practise poured into a Russian vodka bottle, mixed with "exotic juice". They used to drink ethanol eggnogs because Marika got paid in eggs from the farmers; thirty to forty eggs to cure a sick cow. When the salmonella started appearing in the eggs they stopped it, and started mixing the alcohol with juice. I drank that strange and ravaging mixture with them, and at midnight we went to the bar by the harbour, open all night now for drinking and dancing. Somebody, I think it was Ets, bought a bottle of Georgian champagne, and we drank that, too. Some strangers turned up—a pale man with green eyes and a sandy moustache, and a young couple with a Doberman. They were from President Meri's staff—he had a *dacha* on the peninsula, from the Soviet era. I had come across it by chance—a seemingly abandoned narrow dirt road broadened, then turned into an asphalt road, ending by a high gate and a fence. People were dancing wild Estonian waltzes and polkas; under the influence of ethanol and Georgian champagne, the strangers seemed like friends. Dusk merged with dawn, and I walked home, alone.

A few days before this I had gone sailing with Ets and some other people—he owned, I was surprised to learn, a sailing boat. In the middle of the night we anchored outside a small island, and rowed to land. There was a hostel, with old rooms lined in pine, and a bar lit by candles. There was no electricity. A young man came in, tall, willowy, and completely naked. We sat by a rough wooden table, drinking Russian vodka and eating salted cucumber and pickled mushrooms. A woman with long black hair was sleeping on a bench. The candle on our table flickered in the night breeze. The naked young man sat opposite us by the bar, one knee drawn up under his chin, a thin face, with a wispy blond beard. I watched him like a being from another world.

Ets talked about Sweden, and about drinking Swedish coffee on his first visit there, in 1989. The coffee was so strong, he said, that for the first night he didn't sleep at all, his heart racing. I felt unexpectedly tender towards him at the thought of the clean sharp reality of a Swedish bed, his heart racing late at night from the strong Swedish coffee. I wondered what it was like—everything here was so well used compared to Sweden. You lived lightly on it. I wondered, but didn't ask, if he was frightened. "Did you like it?" I asked, finally, and he looked at me, eyes very blue in his tanned face, and said, "Yes, of course," with a quiet kind of emphasis, as if it would be impossible not to like something so rich and clean and beautiful.

"Tell me about London," he said then. "Tell me anything." I told him how you have to drive for hours to get through it, how hot and humid it is in the summer, how you then notice how international London is, how you move quickly through the streets.

We, too, slept on the benches that night, woken by the hostel keeper early the next morning. It was so hot. We swam from the boat, and for a long time I stayed in the water, towed on a rope through the dirty, brackish Baltic Sea.

Who was I at this point, for them? A kind of mascot, perhaps. In the plenty of Estonian summer I was offered strawberries, goose-berries, rides in Ladas. Once I was offered fish, two tiny brown fish. I was always offered drinks, too many drinks. A slight anxiety was setting in about leaving. At the same time the heat, the relentless heatwave made me feel that nothing would ever change. The glaring light was eating me up, and I longed for grey clouds and cool winds. Something felt stuck in my throat. I slept and slept. My Swedish duvet, so warm in the winter, smelled of sweat now. There was no wind—the village echoed without the perennial wind. The dogs howled. I woke up at night from the howling, or from Karl crying next door. The moths fluttered in the kitchen as I stumbled out for a glass of water. I dreamt, anxiously, about leaving my laptop behind.

One day, while taking notes from some of Ivar's files, I heard a scratching at the door, and the softest knock imaginable. It was Ruth, of course, with that carefulness that made her talk always in a whisper and knock so softly, so that the neighbours wouldn't hear. She brought me a finished notebook, her new tract of writing. She also brought me some flowers—small, chubby blue-and-white cushions threaded on a stem. I suspected they might be rare. On one of them a baby snail sat absolutely still, almost transparent, with a hint of something darker deep inside its body, and the beginnings of a shell on its back. I thought of Katarina, and a walk where we had studied the snails on the road, discussing baby snails, origins and appearance—do snails give live birth like whales, or do they lay eggs?

The moment of leaving was drawing near. I anticipated some emotion—perhaps tears, mingled with embarrassment. The prospect of leaving—how to say goodbye—unnerved me, and at the same time I thought a lot about the moment of sitting in the car, self-contained, on my way to Tallinn; freedom, and the end.

I first said goodbye to Ruth. I went into her mosquito-ridden garden. Knocking on her door, I suddenly saw her outside, completely naked with a bucket of water—she was washing. She saw me, and came dancing up, still naked. "It's so hot, so hot," she said, ushering me in to wait for her. Eventually she came in herself in a thin cotton dress. We talked a little, and she sang and prayed for me.

I went on to Ivar. He, too, was practically naked, wearing only some worn-out red-and-white cotton underwear. I don't think he minded that. We said the usual things about keeping in touch, and so on, but I somehow felt we wouldn't. It was so hot. We didn't shake hands.

Alar carried all my things down to the car. I'd already given him and Heli what I wasn't taking. I hugged him, and Heli, and Karl. They gave me a bottle of the 96 percent ethanol to remember them by, a characteristically complex and ironic present. Some men were working on a car in front of the block opposite, including Toivo, the gamekeeper. I waved at him. I was sitting in the car when Ets suddenly walked by. I got out, ignored his outstretched hand, kissed him on the cheek, got in the car, and left. I drove around the building, and looked back. Ets had drifted over to the men by the car. I waved, and just then he turned around and waved, too. I don't know why I kissed him—perhaps I had already left the village culture at the moment of leaving, and come back to myself.

In Tallinn, Veevi was in a blue-and-white-striped house coat. "Look what I have on underneath," she said, hitching it up to show that she, too, was naked. The heat was intense. She made me take a cold shower before lunch, and another one before we left for the harbour, which was blissful. We had a final conversation about her old house. She had sold it by now, but there were other difficulties. She had taken the money out of the country, to Finland, and there were unspecified and unforeseen "complications" at the bank.

She came with me to the harbour. We lost our way, just like my initial visit when she came with me to the airport. Then we found it. I put my car in the queue for the ferry, we said goodbye, and she left. I was sitting in the car waiting, when suddenly a figure loomed, knocking loudly on the window. I jumped and screamed, but it was her, of course. I can't remember why she came back. It must have been some last thing she wanted me to know. Then I sat in the car, self-contained, irrevocably leaving. I put on some lipstick. A man in a green Mercedes next to me was drinking a beer.

That day, on a field near Tallinn, I had seen a large grey dog, like an Alsatian but slightly bigger, with dark-tipped ears, looking like a wolf. Perhaps it was a wolf. On the overnight ferry to Stockholm I dreamt about wolves, a whole pack of them, on that same field, beautiful, and slightly frightening.

And that was it. From Stockholm I went straight to Vienna to see my sister and her husband. I stayed with them at the Hotel Sacher. Thus the morning after leaving the collective farm I was lying in bed, propped up by an impossibly soft bolster and large cushions, a cup of strong coffee with hot milk on the table next to me. A chandelier was hanging from the ornate ceiling, and the pale blue-and-gold silk curtains matched the blue-and-gold wallpaper.

Next to my coffee was a tiny little Sachertorte wrapped in gold foil. The contrast with the collective farm was surreal.

We went, that day, on a tour of the Kunstmuseum to see the newly restored Dürer altarpiece. We saw large Tintorettos on burgundy cloth, Brueghels and Brueghel copyists. The smell of paint was lovely. It was so hot still. A woman copyist had taken off her shoes, painting barefoot in that splendid room.

In the evening, going back to the hotel in a taxi, the driver playing loud romantic music, streetlights flickering by, I was filled with a new sense of potential, of leisure and luxury. I was also still floating in an in-between world, losing the primary purpose that had kept me on the collective farm for a year. Having kept a diary for a year, I could now no longer write—everything I wrote seemed contrived and inauthentic. And having worried so much about losing my laptop, I very nearly walked away from it at the airport in Stockholm. A kind stranger alerted me to the padded bag on the trolley, after I had taken several steps away from it. He smiled and shook his head at me, not knowing, of course, that a year's work, and the PhD and book to come, was in that laptop.

On 11 August Daniel Miller had written his last letter to me on the collective farm:

> I am genuinely delighted with the way that it has end up for you. I cannot believe that an ethnographic field experience that has gone so well would not produce equally successful academic results. I am also very pleased that the subjective experience of seeing your own identity through the field situation has become in itself such a positive force in helping you empathise with the experience of otherness amongst those with whom you have been living.

He ended:

Above all I note the remark that you are thinking of living there. I know this is but fantasy but it suggests the kind of empathy and involvement which an ethnography is supposed to rest upon. It is exactly what a supervisor would want to hear in the last letter from an ethnographer. I am very glad indeed that the experience has been so worthwhile.

How strange it all was.

On 1 September I was back in my flat in Hampstead. I rearranged my books, both restless and pleased to be back. Everything seemed so easy, still, and would for a long time to come.

That first night back I dreamt that there was a trapped swallow in a room. I caught it, carefully, and held it. I felt its heart beating. Then I released it.

That was the end.

Afterword

Some ten years after I left the village, I came back for a visit, with Eric, my husband. We flew in from Helsinki, over thin brown ice. I had a sudden imaginary whiff of what Estonia used to smell like—brown coal, and stale poverty. The airport had been renovated, and now had a gleaming grey granite floor, and luggage trolleys with adverts for mobile phones: NOKIA EMT—DON'T LEAVE HOME WITHOUT THEM. I sensed a slight whiff, again, of that smell. Was it real, or was it a sensory hallucination? There were more adverts, everywhere, for KPMG, for Reval Hotels. I thought of my Soviet textbooks on the collective farm:

> When you come to New York you will see lots of cars, big and small, black and yellow, old and modern. You will also see and hear advertisements everywhere. They fill the newspapers and cover the walls. They are shouted through loudspeakers and shown in the cinemas.

My Nokia cell phone registered an Estonian network. We stood by the luggage carousel and waited, until it became clear that my suitcase wouldn't arrive. Later we tried to change some money. Three young Swedes were queuing in front of us. It was morning, and they were drunk. "You can't fall in love with them," one of them said, insistently, but also slightly experimentally, "fucking hell, don't sit there for hours kissing them—you can't fall in love with a whore." I stiffened behind them; they didn't know I could understand them. They stood close together, tall, loud, and vaguely threatening. Eric didn't understand the Swedish, but disapproved nevertheless, disdainful of their drunkenness. It was an awful combination, the drunk young Swedes, the degrading conversation, the gleaming floors, and the adverts.

Outside the airport was a new shopping centre, Prisma, and new, lit-up adverts everywhere. It was a new city, with shining glass buildings. It has to be said that it was hideous, the new capitalism. Hotel Viru was completely reconstructed, with garish, cheap luxury. We were on the "business" floor. Inside, however, it was not so bad, and not completely unlike what it was. Eric bustled, arranging our things, taking calls on his mobile. I sat eating salted peanuts from a tin. The moon in the darkening sky was full and yellow, half covered in a black cloud. I sat there by the window for a long time, listening to the trams, and the new traffic. Eric walked naked through the room, the post-Soviet room. He handed me his mobile phone on the way to the shower. "If somebody rings . . ." he said. "I answer," I said, filled with this new gesture of intimacy, of trust. We were so newly married, still.

We woke up late the following morning, and suddenly it didn't feel so exciting anymore. There had been a heavy beat in the night from Café Amigo, the new hotel nightclub. Across the square was Venus Club, emitting its own light and music. I sat for a while that morning, in the same place, looking out over the sea. Eric walked by, not looking at me, trying not to disturb me. I was writing notes, and looking at the vast black hulls at sea.

Later we walked through the beautiful town centre of Tallinn. There were only a few unrenovated houses left, all the flaking facades from the Soviet times painted and restored. Suddenly an Estonian woman asked us for money: a respectable person, maybe sixty years old, in a beret and good shoes. I looked at her in amazement; Eric, firmly, said no. Tinny music spilled onto the street, she walked on, as did we.

Later we set off for Haapsalu in a rented car. I remembered the way, more or less. The road was flawless, lined with huge signs at regular intervals: THIS ROAD HAS BEEN REBUILT WITH THE AID OF THE EU RECONSTRUCTION FUND. I saw a stork nest, and the forest looked much as it was, except for the new telecom masts dotting the landscape. We had a full mobile signal everywhere; it seems obvious now, but then it was not. About halfway we stopped for a picnic of oatcakes, sheep's cheese, apples, and dark chocolate. Eric suggested wine; I refused.

We were getting closer, crossing into the peninsula. Many of the farmhouses were red now, that symbolic Swedish red. Even one of the old milk stands on the road was painted red. We passed the church, and then the old shop, which had closed down. The old dairy was being renovated. The stork nest was still there, resting on the tall chimney. We passed a sign to a new museum, LYCKHOLM, and then we drove into the village.

There we were. The square was the same. The ground around the blocks of flats was dug up; it looked like the work had come to a standstill. There was also, unexpectedly, graffiti on the wall of the old workshops, a yellow, pink, and red design. The village actually looked poorer than it had been, except for the manor house, which had been renovated, and rented rooms.

We stayed there. As I wrote notes, Eric was lying on the bed looking mildly unhappy, holding our room key (JOIN THE NAVY. SEE THE WORLD on the key chain.) Then Alar and Heli came by, and were exactly themselves, but more confident, and happier. They showed me the school. The whiff of urine, I noticed, was gone: the new lavatories were Swedish. And it was warm.

I asked them about the graffiti. It turns out to have been a school project—the students wanted to make the village less grey, and got permission to do it, made sketches, and then painted the graffiti. I had assumed a story of rebellion, and in fact it turned out to be a cosily communal, even a creative, story.

Before dinner we drove to the new nature reserve. There was a replica of a Sami hut, and a birdwatching tower, and many empty bottles of vodka in the grass. But the light, still, was ethereal, blue, pink, and purple. White young birch and reeds stretched for miles; the water in the sea inlet was still as a pond, with a thin skin of ice near the shore. Birds of early spring were calling in that cold blue dusk. I longed to see an elk, like a physical desire.

The next day we met Ets as we were having lunch—a small blond man coming into the kitchen, looking for something. He didn't recognise me.

"Ets?" I said.

"Yes, I am Ets," he said enquiringly.

"I am Sigrid," I said.

"Oooh," he said, a long oooh, and then he hugged me, gently, Swedish style. He looked at me intently when Eric left the room. "I remember your eyes," he said quite unexpectedly.

That was in 2003. I think, now, ten years later, about the Estonian poet Jaan Kaplinski:

If I Wanted to Go Back

If I wanted to go back
I should know that the thoughts
I thought going through the empty houses
are as empty as the houses
where moths gnaw and fungus eats
the walls and where the spinning wheel stands alone
in the corner, where the spade stands alone
before the threshold. This emptiness is great indeed,
as is the land. Each one is someone else
from everywhere and leads the way

somewhere else, and no one could ever
walk through all this land:
every beginning is different after its end
than it was before it ended, and everything is always
something else: the houses remain empty
and I haven't the strength, nobody has the strength
to live and die with everyone,
to step across your thresholds, sleep in all your beds.
(Translated from the Estonian by Sam Hamill)

The thoughts I thought going through the empty houses are as empty as the houses. The empty houses, that distorted nostalgia I felt. What was I nostalgic for? I wonder now. Not my lost home, but my lost homeland. *This emptiness is great indeed, as is the land.* Ah yes: the emptiness, the land. *I haven't the strength, nobody has the strength to live and die with everyone, to step across your thresholds, sleep in all your beds.* Did I do enough? Did I stay for long enough? I hope so. This, I know, is not the only story that could have been told of that time, about those people and that place.

Every beginning is different after its end. Everything is always something else.

Timeline

13th–14th Century	The first Swedish farmers and fishermen settle in Estonia.
1561	Northern Estonia submits to the Swedish Crown, whilst Southern Estonia forms the Duchy of Livonia under the control of the Lithuanian Duchy and the Polish Crown.
1629	All of Estonia becomes part of the Swedish Crown.
1721	Sweden loses Estonia to Russia in the peace treaty of Nystad, following the Great Northern War (1700–1721).
1862	The Estonian national epic, *Kalevipoeg*, is collated and published.
1918	The Estonian Declaration of Independence is issued but not accepted by the newly established Soviet regime. War on two fronts, against Russia and Germany.
1920	The Tartu Peace Treaty is signed. Parliamentary democracy is established.
1934	President Konstantin Päts stages an authoritarian coup to undermine the extreme right-wing Vaps movement.

August 1939	The secret protocol to the Molotov-Ribbentrop Pact is signed, in effect dividing eastern Europe into Russian and German spheres of interest.
16 June 1940	The USSR invades Estonia. Ninety thousand Red Army troops enter the country the following day. The Estonian government capitulates.
6 August 1940	The Estonian Soviet Republic is established.
14 June 1941	First Soviet mass deportations from Estonia.
28 August 1941	Tallinn is occupied by Nazi forces. Estonia is incorporated into the German province of Ostland. Jews are rounded up and killed. Several concentration camps and killing sites are established.
January 1944	The Red Army pushes back into Estonia. By autumn Estonia is under Soviet control.
Summer 1944	The Estonian Swedes are evacuated to Sweden by local SS officers, in return for payment.
March 1949	Second Soviet mass deportations from Estonia.
1953	Joseph Stalin dies. Some Gulag prisoners are freed and rehabilitated.
1961/62	First and second Soviet Holocaust trials in Tallinn and Tartu.
1989	The Singing Revolution. A human chain of more than two million people, stretching from Estonia, through Latvia, and

into Lithuania, is formed to protest against Soviet rule.

20 August 1991 Estonian independence is declared.

26 December 1991 The Soviet Union is formally dissolved.

31 August 1994 The last Russian troops leave Estonia.

October 1998 President Lennart Meri sets up the Estonian International Commission for Investigation of Crimes Against Humanity.

1 May 2004 Estonia accedes to the European Union after a referendum in September 2003 shows 66.8 percent support.

2008 The Estonian International Commission is succeeded by the Estonian Institute of Historical Memory, established by President Toomas Hendrik Ilves.

Acknowledgments

I would like to thank all the people who make an appearance in this book, particularly Alar and Hele Uus, Ivar Rüütli, Inna and Toivo Hammerberg, Ülo, Kalm, and Laine Belovas.

Ruth Kanarbik and Veevi Kirschbaum are sadly no longer alive. They both, in their own ways, contributed a great deal to this book, and I want to acknowledge their generosity.

Professor Daniel Miller, who was my PhD supervisor, was always supportive, and has consented to being quoted in this book. It was a great privilege to work with him.

Lisbet Rausing, my sister, has read and commented extensively. Her encouragement and advice have been invaluable. Thank you, also, to everyone else in my family—not least my dear husband, Eric Abraham.

Finally, I want to thank my publisher, Morgan Entrekin, and my patient and meticulous editor, Peter Blackstock, for taking on this book, and for handling it so well.

This book is dedicated to my parents, Hans and Märit Rausing. Thank you for everything.